Math in Art, and Art in Math

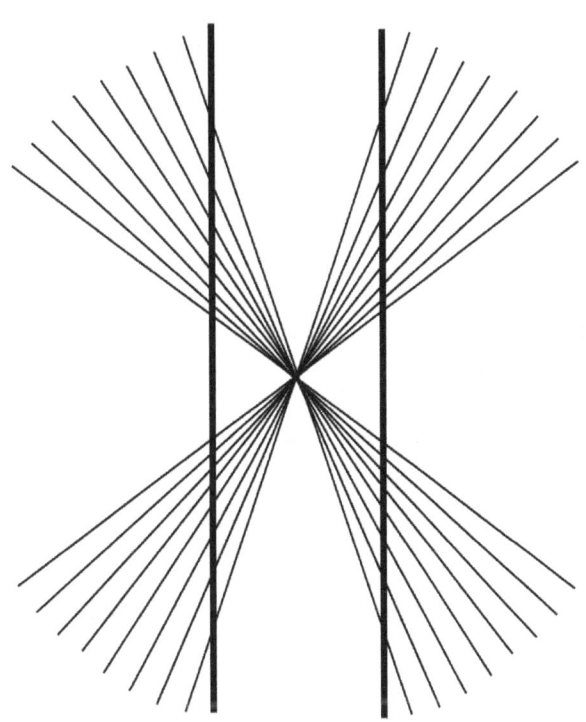

by **Stephen Fratini**

Table of Contents

List of Figures

Preface

This is the fourth book that I have written. Like most authors (of just about any type of book), a preface is started before the book is written and then updated after the book is mostly complete. At least for me, the initial intent and end result of my books have not been an exact match. So, I thought it would be interesting for the reader to see my intent before I actually started to write and my summary of what I had actually written. To this end, the preface that follows is divided into two parts.

Preface written before I've started to write the book:

This book is about art and mathematics. There are several facets to be considered, i.e., art that has a mathematical foundation (e.g., mosaics), mathematics that is applied to art (e.g., perspective) and mathematics that results in things that most would consider pleasing to view (e.g., abstract tessellations and computer generated fractal images). Other things are harder to classify but nevertheless embody aspects of mathematics and art (e.g., optical illusions).

The intent is to keep the mathematical detail at a minimum or at least make it easy for the reader to skip the mathematical details if they wish.

Preface written after the book was mostly complete:

Well, I'm back after having written a draft of this book and am happy to say that I've pretty much kept to my initial intent. I've even kept to my planned set of major sections, i.e., tilings and tessellations, perspective, optical illusions, patterns, fractals, and proofs without words.

The focus here is on a subset of art, i.e., painting, architecture and textiles. Mathematics is also related to other forms of art such as music, dance and sculpture, but these aspects are not covered in this book.

The mathematical details have been kept to a minimum, as I had hope to do when I started writing. All you need to read this book is an understanding of some basic geometry and algebra.

The sections are to a large extent independent, with very few cross references among the sections. So, feel free to jump into the book wherever you have an interest.

There are many references in this book (most relating to topics for further study by the reader). I've made extensive use of Wikipedia, YouTube and other online resources. These external references (especially the YouTube videos) are essential extensions of the book. In particular, the reader is encouraged to check-out the videos.

Perhaps something of a warning – I am a trained mathematician and have very limited art skills (while I do love art). Please keep this in mind when reading the book.

In places where I state an opinion, I start my comment with "**Author's Remark**"; otherwise, I've tried to stick to the facts.

Acknowledgements

The author would like to thank Laura Bagwell, Michel Besson and Tony Clark for their helpful comments and review of this book.

Stephen Fratini
Sole Proprietor of The Art of Managing Things
Eatontown, New Jersey (USA)
Email: sfratini@artofmanagingthings.com
LinkedIn: www.linkedin.com/in/stephenfratini

Other books by the author:

- *The Art of Managing Things (2nd edition)*, self-published on Amazon, https://www.amazon.com/Art-Managing-Things-Stephen-Fratini-ebook/dp/B07N4H4YWH/, January 2019.

- *Mathematical Thinking: Exercises for the Mind*, self-published on Amazon, https://www.amazon.com/Mathematical-Thinking-Exercises-Stephen-Fratini-ebook/dp/B08F75CDD6/, August 2020.

- *Financial Mathematics with Python*, self-published on Amazon, https://www.amazon.com/gp/product/B08VKQR141, February 2021.

1   Introduction

1.1   Purpose

The purpose of this book is to introduce the reader to some of the many interrelationships between mathematics and art. This is neither a mathematics book nor an art book in the sense that the intent is not to provide mathematics or art lessons. The goal is to leave the reader with a deeper appreciation of the synergies between the two subjects, and a desire to explore further.

1.2   Intended Audience

This book is intended for the general public. As noted below, the prerequisites are minimal.

1.3   Prerequisites

High school level algebra and geometry are the main requirements regarding math.

With regard to art, no specific art talent is required other than a general appreciation of art.

1.4   Outline

It is recommended to read Sections 1 and 2 first. The remaining sections can be read in any order.

Section 1 is this introduction.

Section 2 provides a brief history of the interrelationships between mathematics and art.

Section 3 covers tilings and tessellations.

Section 4 is about perspective in art, with a brief foray into perspective geometry (one of the more technical parts of the book).

Section 5 provides many examples of optical illusions.

Section 6 is a miscellaneous collection of various patterns that did not fit easily into the other sections of the book.

Section 7 contains an overview of fractals.

Section 8 covers something called "proofs without words", basically mathematical proofs that are expressed with one or just a few figures, and require limited or no explanation.

2 Historical Perspective

The relationship between art and mathematics goes much further back than recorded history. Recent research has found geometric symbols in ancient cave paintings. In 2007, paleoanthropologist Genevieve von Petzinger embarked on a study of geometric signs found in caves and other sites, dating back as far as 40,000 years ago during the Stone Age, see [1] and [2]. While the ancient cave paintings are best known for drawings of animals and humans, the geometric signs far outnumber the animal and human images. Some of the geometric symbols discovered by von Petzinger in ice age Europe are shown in Figure 1. She compares the symbols to modern day emojis.

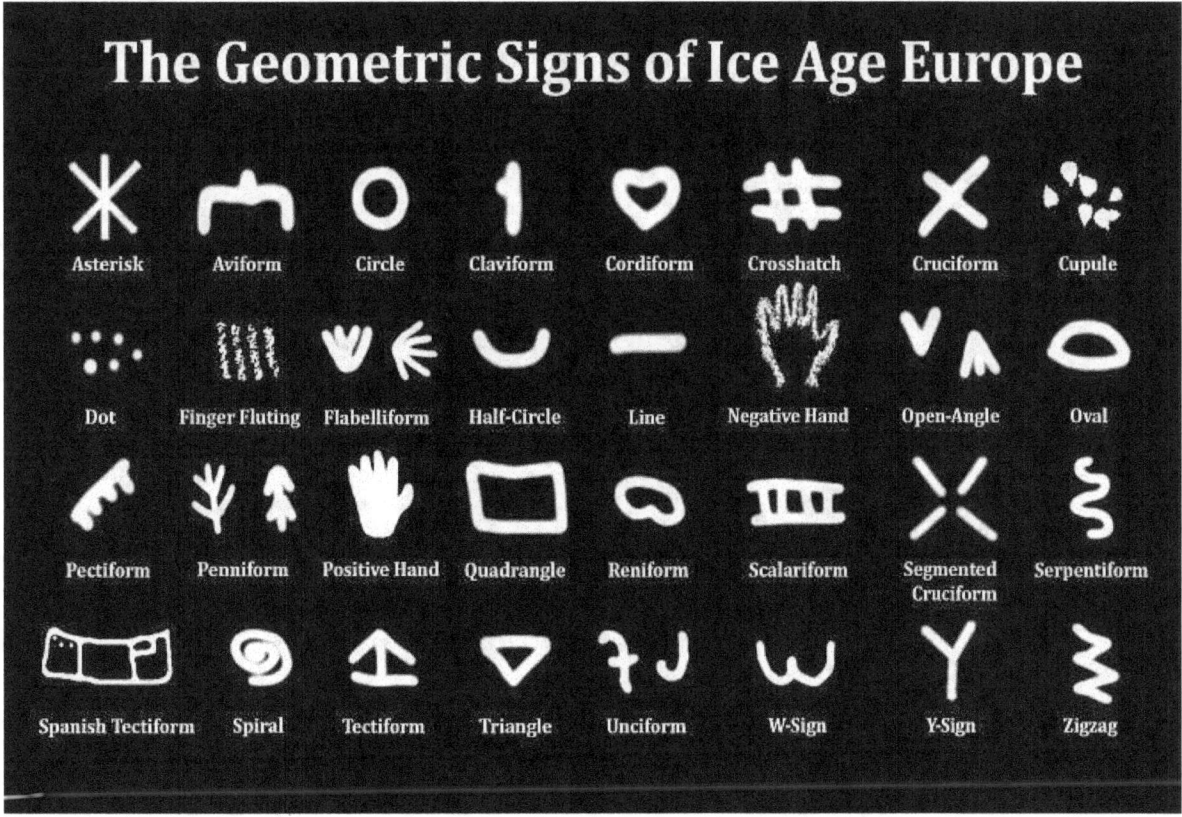

Figure 1. Geometric symbols in ancient cave paintings

Tessellations (which are discussed in Section 3) can be traced to the Sumerian civilization (about 4000 B.C.), in which building walls were decorated by tiling designs constructed from clay [3]. Figure 2 shows a geometric mosaic from Basilica of St. Eufemia in Grado, Friuli-Venezia Giulia, Italy. The basilica is famous for the incredibly well preserved 6th century A.D. mosaics that decorate the basilica's floor, as it is extremely rare to find the original floor mosaics preserved in such an early Christian basilica.

Figure credits to Wolfgang Sauber, see
https://commons.wikimedia.org/wiki/File:Grado_St.Eufemia_-_Geometrisches_Mosaik_5.jpg.

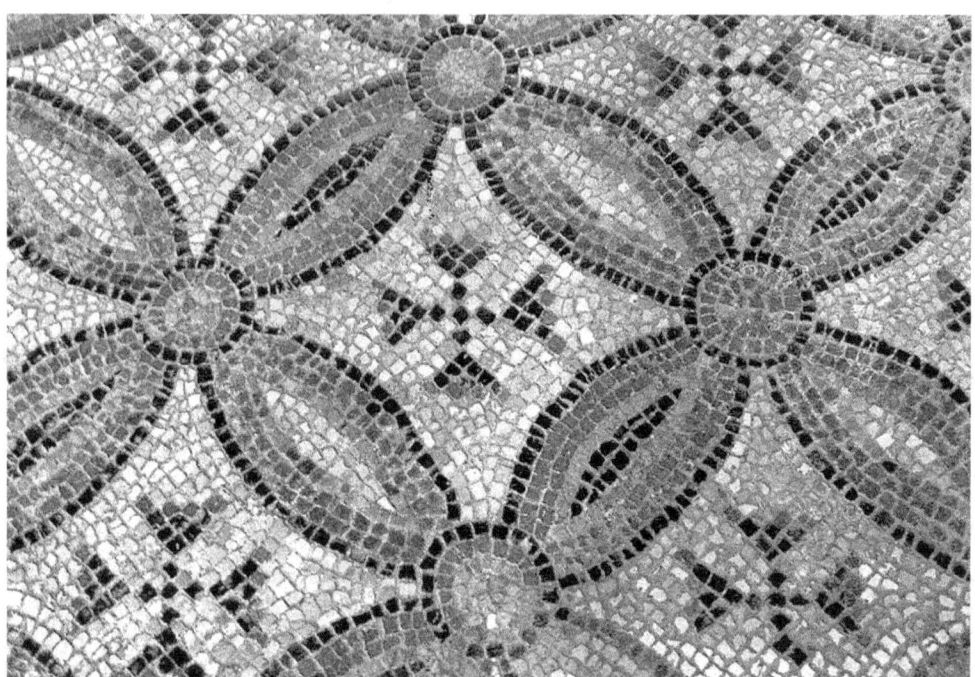

Figure 2. Mosaic from Basilica of St. Eufemia

The exploration of perspective in art and its association with mathematics has a long history. As noted in the Wikipedia article on perspective [29]:

> Systematic attempts to evolve a system of perspective are usually considered to have begun around the fifth century B.C. in the art of ancient Greece, as part of a developing interest in illusionism allied to theatrical scenery. This was detailed within Aristotle's *Poetics* as skenographia: using flat panels on a stage to give the illusion of depth. The philosophers Anaxagoras and Democritus worked out **geometric theories of perspective** for use with skenographia …

> Filippo Brunelleschi conducted a series of experiments between 1415 and 1420, which included making drawings of various Florentine buildings in correct perspective …

> Soon after Brunelleschi's demonstrations, nearly every artist in Florence and in Italy used geometrical perspective in their paintings and sculpture, notably Donatello, Masaccio, Lorenzo Ghiberti, Masolino da Panicale, Paolo Uccello, and Filippo Lippi …

> As shown by the quick proliferation of accurate perspective paintings in Florence, Brunelleschi likely understood (with help from his friend the mathematician Toscanelli), but did not publish the mathematics behind perspective. Decades later, his friend Leon Battista Alberti wrote *De pictura* (c. 1435), a treatise on proper methods of showing distance in painting. Alberti's primary breakthrough was not to show the mathematics in terms of conical projections, as it actually appears to the eye. Instead, he formulated the theory based on planar projections, or how the rays of light, passing from the viewer's eye to the landscape, would strike the picture plane (the painting). He was then able to calculate the apparent height of a distant object using two similar triangles. The mathematics behind similar triangles is relatively simple, having been long ago formulated by Euclid. Alberti was also trained in the science of optics through the school of Padua and under the influence of Biagio Pelacani da Parma who studied Alhazen's *Book of Optics*. This book, translated around 1200 A.D. into Latin, had laid the mathematical foundation for perspective in Europe.

The topic of perspective is discussed further in Section 4 of this book.

Moving closer to the present, fractals are self-similar objects (i.e., infinitely repeating with finer and finer levels of detail) that are often used in abstract artwork. While fractals predate the advent of the electronic computer, the availability of computer graphics has led to an explosion of fractal art. Figure 3 is a computer generated spiral fractal. Fractals are covered further in Section 7 of this book.

Figure credits are to Jahobr, see https://commons.wikimedia.org/wiki/File:Spiral_of_black_and_white_squares_10_till_repetition_zooming_in.gif. Also, at the above link, there is also an animated version of the fractal which highlights the infinitely repeating pattern as one zooms into the center of the figure.

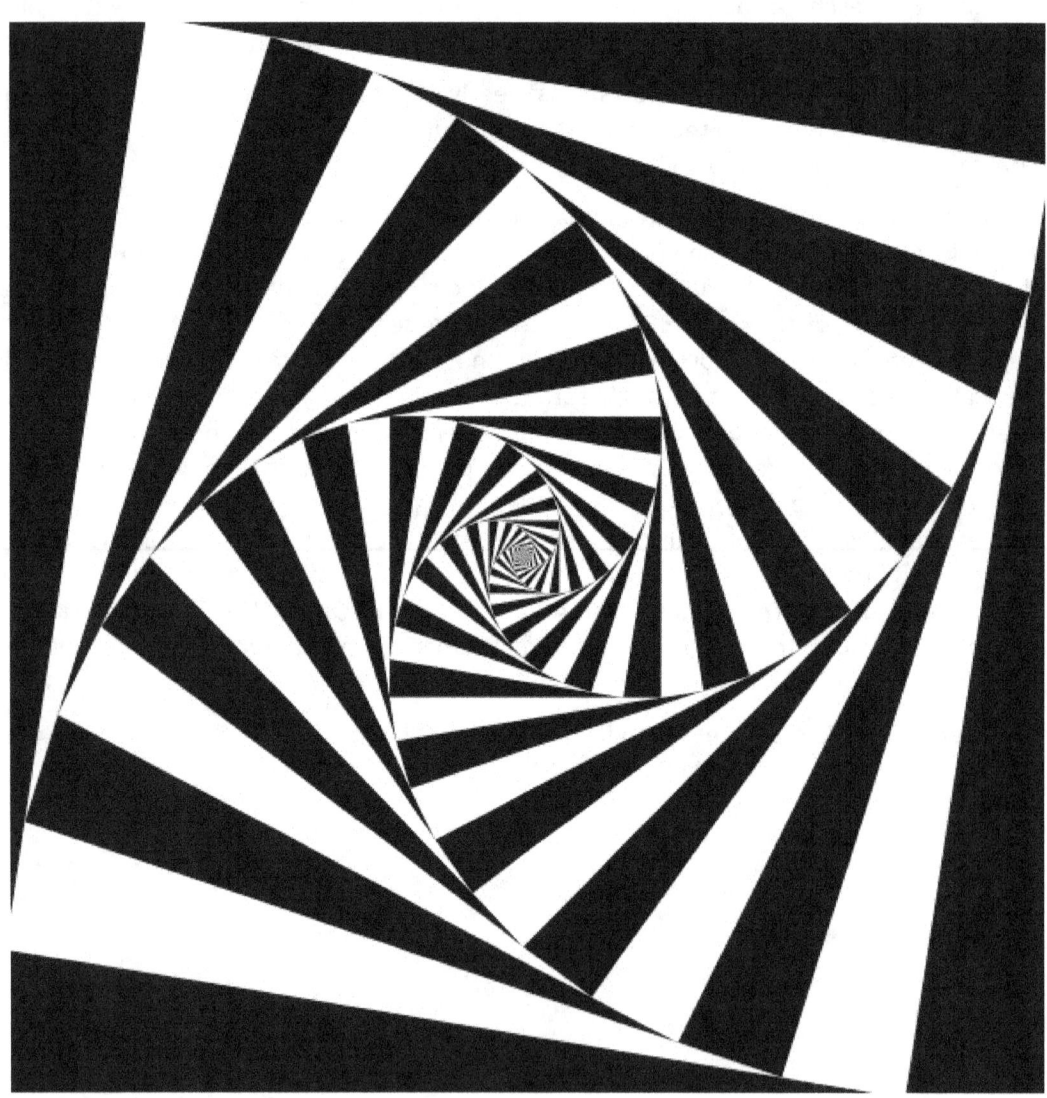

Figure 3. Spiral fractal

Abstract art is in many cases highly mathematical, e.g.,

- Jackson Pollock's artworks from his "drip period" are essentially fractal in nature. For example, see Pollock's Number 1 (Lavender Mist), 1950 [4].

- Piet Mondrian's grid-based paintings are highly geometrical. For example, see Mondrian's Composition No.10, 1939-1942 [5].

- Theo van Doesburg's "Composition in gray (Rag Time)" is another example of geometrical art, see Figure 4 (for credits, see https://www.wikiart.org/en/theo-van-doesburg/composition-in-gray-rag-time-1919).

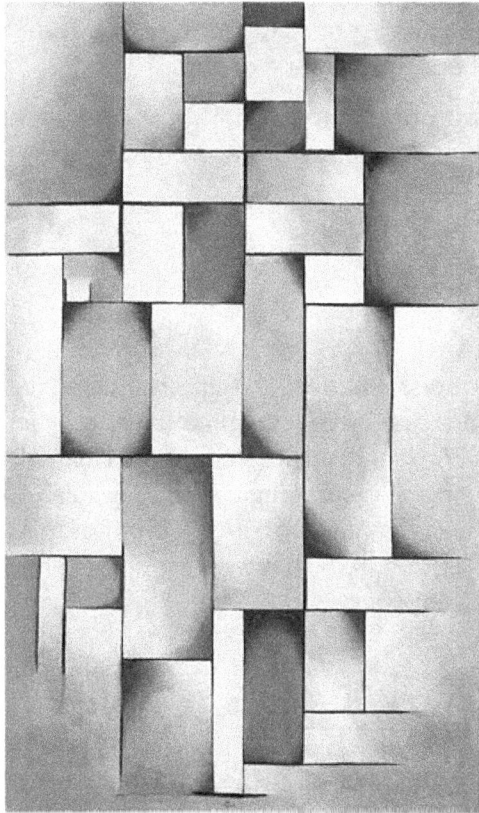

Figure 4. Composition in gray (Rag Time), 1919

. . .

This section has covered just a few snippets from the history of art and mathematics. For a more complete accounting of the relationships between art and mathematics, see the Wikipedia article entitled "Mathematics and art" [6].

3   Tilings and Tessellations

3.1   Overview

A **tessellation** or **tiling** is a pattern comprised of one or more shapes such that the shapes fit together without any gaps or overlaps. Without qualification, the concept typically refers to flat (planar) shapes, but the concept can be extended to higher dimensions. In terms of language derivations, the Wikipedia article on tessellations [7] states the following:

> In Latin, tessella is a small cubical piece of clay, stone or glass used to make mosaics. The word "tessella" means "small square" (from tessera, square, which in turn is from the Greek word τέσσερα for four). It corresponds to the everyday term tiling, which refers to applications of tessellations, often made of glazed clay.

In what follows, the terms "tessellation" and "tiling" are used interchangeably. Further, keep in mind that, by definition, a tiling of the plane is infinite and as such, only part of each tiling is shown in the figures that follow.

3.2   Classifications

3.2.1   Regular Tessellations

There are many classifications of tessellations. The simplest category is that of tessellations formed by regular polygons, i.e., polygons that are equiangular (all angles are equal in measure) and equilateral (all sides have the same length). These are known as **regular tessellations**. There are only three possible tilings of the plane with a single type of regular polygon – only equilateral triangles, squares and regular hexagons will work (for a proof of this fact, see Regular Tessellation article in Wolfram MathWorld [8]). Figure 5 shows a portion of each type of tiling. The black and white colorings are purely for visual effect.

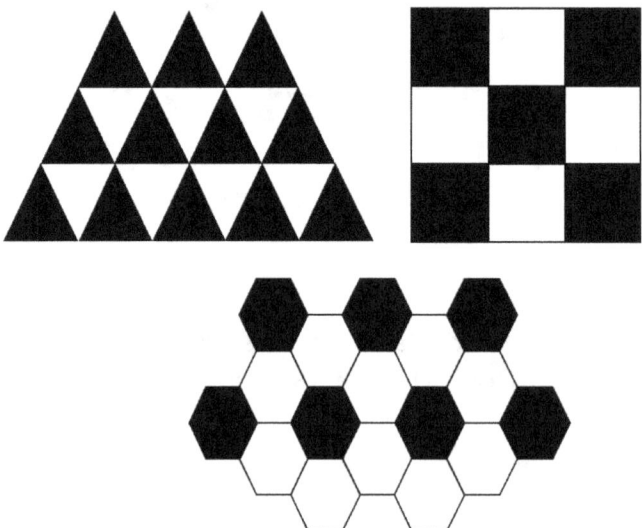

Figure 5. Examples of regular tessellations in the plane

When classifying various types of tessellations, the concept of vertex configuration is very useful. A **vertex configuration** is a sequence of numbers that represents the number of sides on each face surrounding a given vertex. For example, the notation a.b.c.d describes a vertex that has 4 faces surrounding it, with a, b, c and d sides, respectively. In Figure 5, all the vertices in the triangle-based tiling have vertex configuration 3.3.3.3.3.3, all the vertices in the square-based tiling have vertex configuration 4.4.4.4 and all the vertices in the hexagon-based tiling have vertex configuration 6.6.6.

3.2.2   Semi-regular Tessellations

Figure 6, Figure 7, Figure 8 and Figure 9 depict what are called **semi-regular tessellations** (also known as Archimedean or uniform tilings). Semi-regular tessellations are comprised of two or more regular polygons such that all the vertices have the same vertex configuration (shown above each tiling in the figures below). The colorings are for visual effect only.

Figure credits for all the semi-regular tessellations go to Tom Ruen, see the Wikipedia article "Euclidean tilings by convex regular polygons" [11].

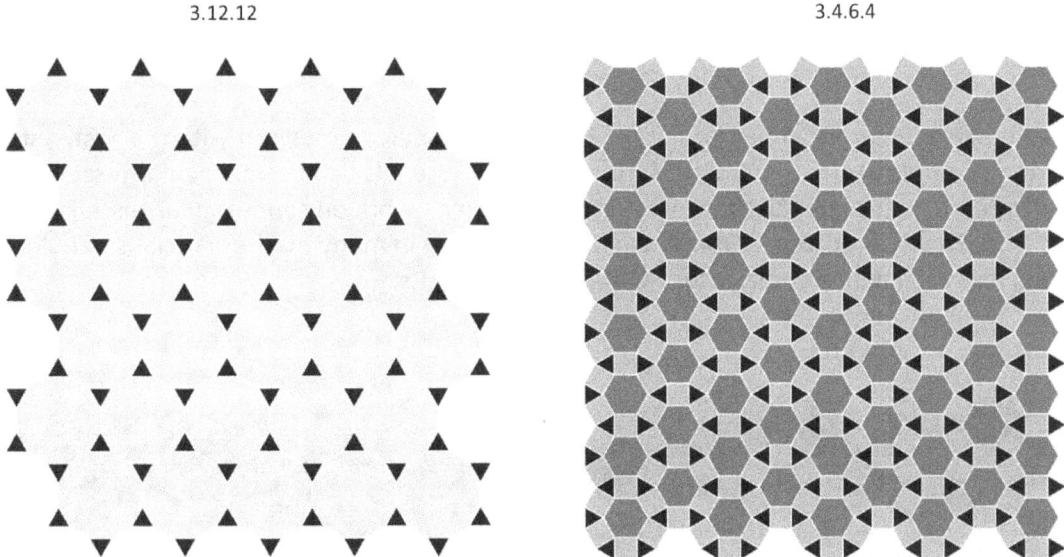

Figure 6. Semi-regular tessellations - Part 1

Surprisingly, there are only 8 possible semi-regular tessellations. A proof of this fact can be found in Section 2.2 of the paper by Swanson [12]. The general idea of the proof is that the interior angles of the regular polygons surrounding a vertex must add to 360 degrees (2π radians) and this only allows for a limited number of possibilities.

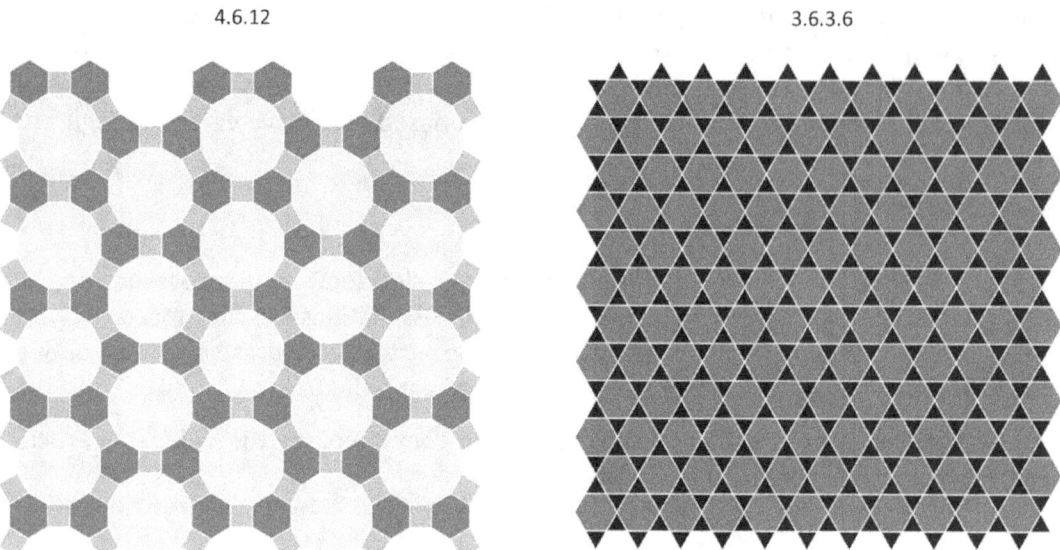

4.6.12   3.6.3.6

Figure 7. Semi-regular tessellations - Part 2

The famous astronomer Johannes Kepler (1571-1630) is generally credited with the first systematic explanation of semi-regular tessellations. He wrote about regular and semi-regular tessellations in his book *Harmonices Mundi* (1619). Unfortunately, Kepler's work on semi-regular tessellations was neglected (perhaps "forgotten" is more accurate), resulting in many mathematicians needlessly replicating his work, and in some cases, with incorrect results.

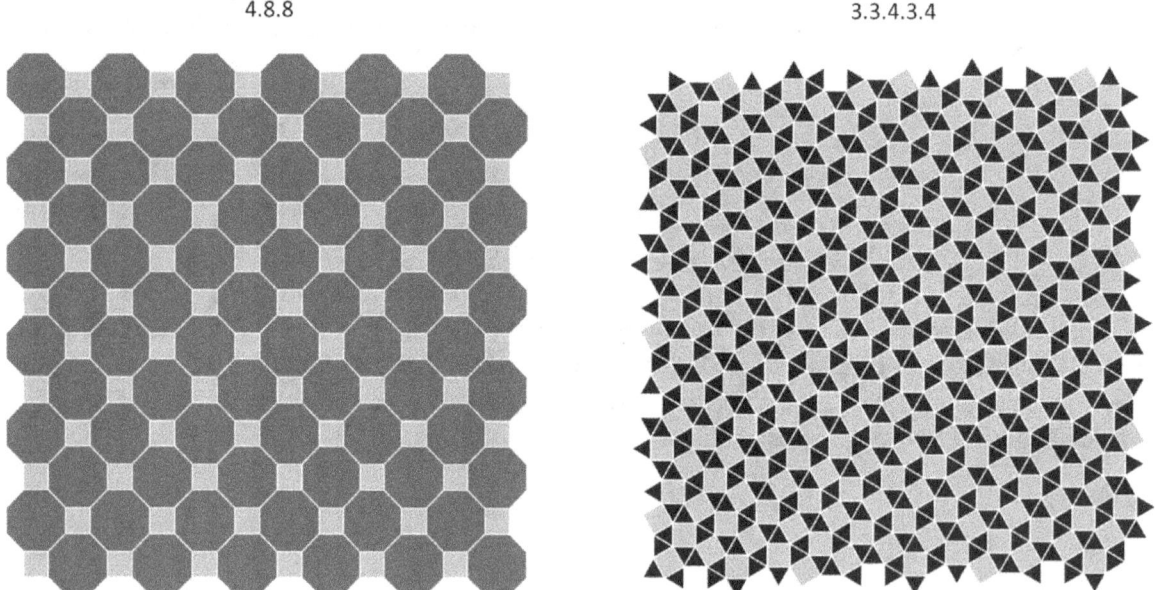

4.8.8   3.3.4.3.4

Figure 8. Semi-regular tessellations - Part 3

An extensive list and associated drawing of many tessellations (including the semi-regular tessellations) can be found in the Wikipedia article entitled *List of tessellations* [9].

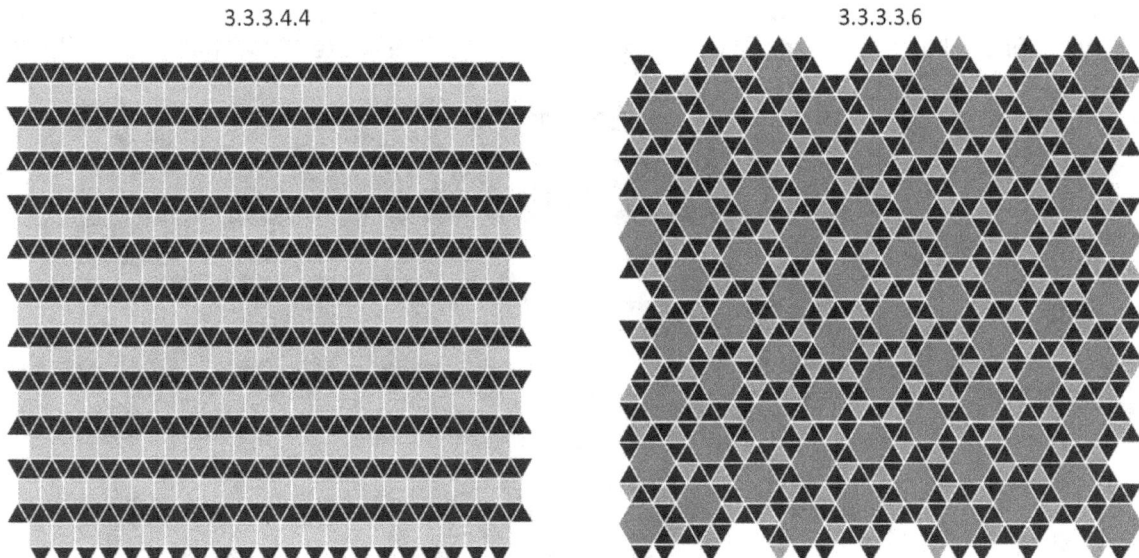

Figure 9. Semi-regular tessellations – Part 4

3.2.3   K-uniform Tessellations

A **k-uniform tessellation** is a tiling of the plane using regular polygons with k different vertex patterns. We've already seen the set of 1-uniform tessellations, i.e., the three regular tilings, and the eight semi-regular tessellations.

Although a bit dated, the paper entitled *Tilings by Regular Polygons* [10] gives a good overview of k-uniform tessellations. The Wikipedia article entitled *Euclidean tilings by convex regular polygons* [11] provides an up-to-date status on k-uniform tessellations and includes many beautifully illustrated examples.

Figure 10 shows an example of a 4-uniform tessellation. The small white circles, at top center of the figure, highlight the four types of vertices. The tessellation is described by the following notation:

$$[3^2.4.3.4; 3^2.6^2; 3.4^2.6; 6^3]$$

The description for each vertex is separated by a semi-colon. The vertex notation is same as that used for semi-regular tessellation with one further compression, i.e., repeats such as 3.3.3.3 are written as 3^4. For example, 6^3 represents the pattern for the vertices surrounded by 3 hexagons in Figure 10. [**Author's remark**: Yes, I could have used the compressed notation for semi-regular tessellations but thought it was better to use the expanded form when first introducing the notation.]

Credits for Figure 10 go to Tom Ruen, https://commons.wikimedia.org/wiki/File:4-uniform_6.svg. The original figure has been changed to grayscale and the 4 small white circles have been added.

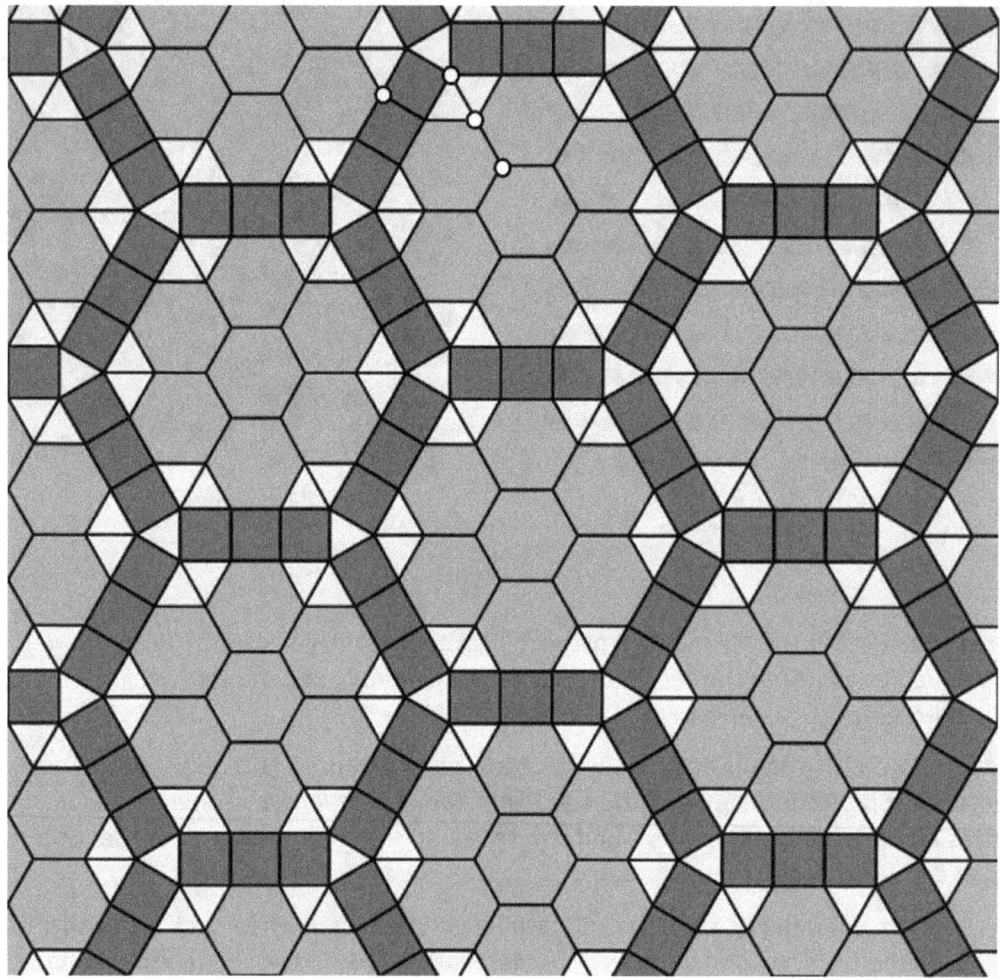

Figure 10. Example of a 4-uniform tessellation

Figure 11 illustrates a complication in the classification scheme regarding k-uniform tessellations, i.e., several vertices of the same type can be situated differently within a tessellation. The tessellation in Figure 11 is considered to be a 3-uniform tessellation even though there are only two different vertices types, i.e., $3.4.6.4$ and $3.4^2.6$. However, the vertices of type 3.4.6.4 are situated within the tessellation in two different ways (see, for example, the two vertices labeled as 1 and 2 in the figure). Another way to view the situation is to imagine a second identical tiling. There is no combination of translations, rotations or reflections that allows one to place the second tiling on top of the first tiling with Vertex #1 placed directly over Vertex #2, while completely aligning the patterns.

An example of a $3.4^2.6$ vertex is covered by the circle with horizontal stripes.

In terms of notation, the tessellation in Figure 11 is represented as $[(3.4.6.4)2; 3.4^2.6]$. The "2" after (3.4.6.4) indicates that the particular vertex type is positioned in two different ways within the tessellation.

Credits for Figure 11 go to Tom Ruen, see https://commons.wikimedia.org/wiki/File:3-uniform_26.svg. The figure has been changed to grayscale, with the addition of three circles to highlight examples of the two types of vertices.

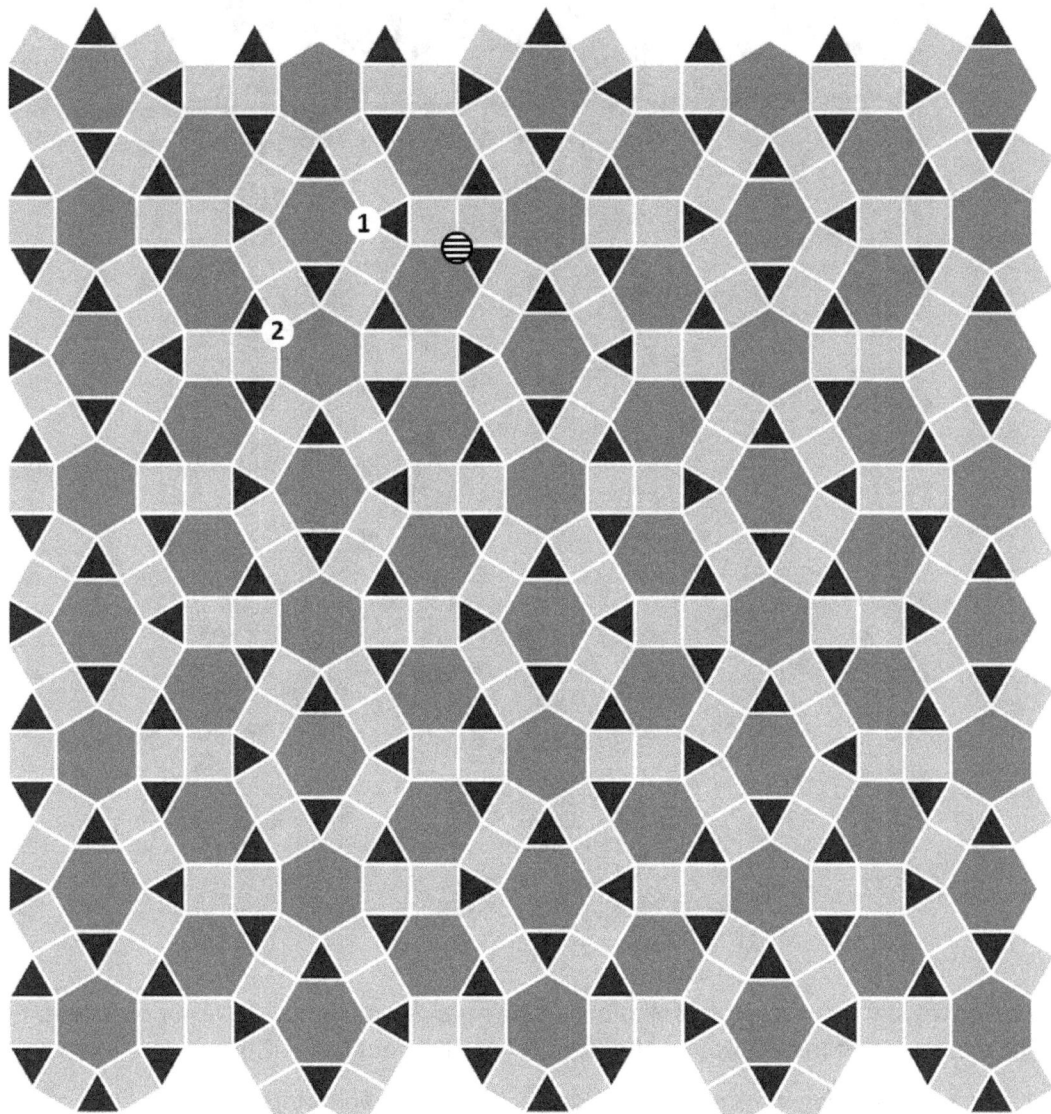

Figure 11. Example of a 3-uniform, 2 vertex type tessellation

Figure 12 depicts a 5-uniform tessellation with only 2 vertex types, i.e., one vertex is of type 4.6.12 and another vertex is of type 3.4.6.4. The vertex of type 3.4.6.4 is situated within the tessellation in four different ways (see the four vertices highlighted with white circles in Figure 12). Notice that each of the white vertices is situated differently with respect to the 12-gon. The vertex notation for this tessellation is [(3.4.6.4)4; 4.6.12].

Credits for Figure 12 go to Tom Ruen, see https://commons.wikimedia.org/wiki/File:5-uniform_36.svg. The original figure has been changed to grayscale and four small circles have been added.

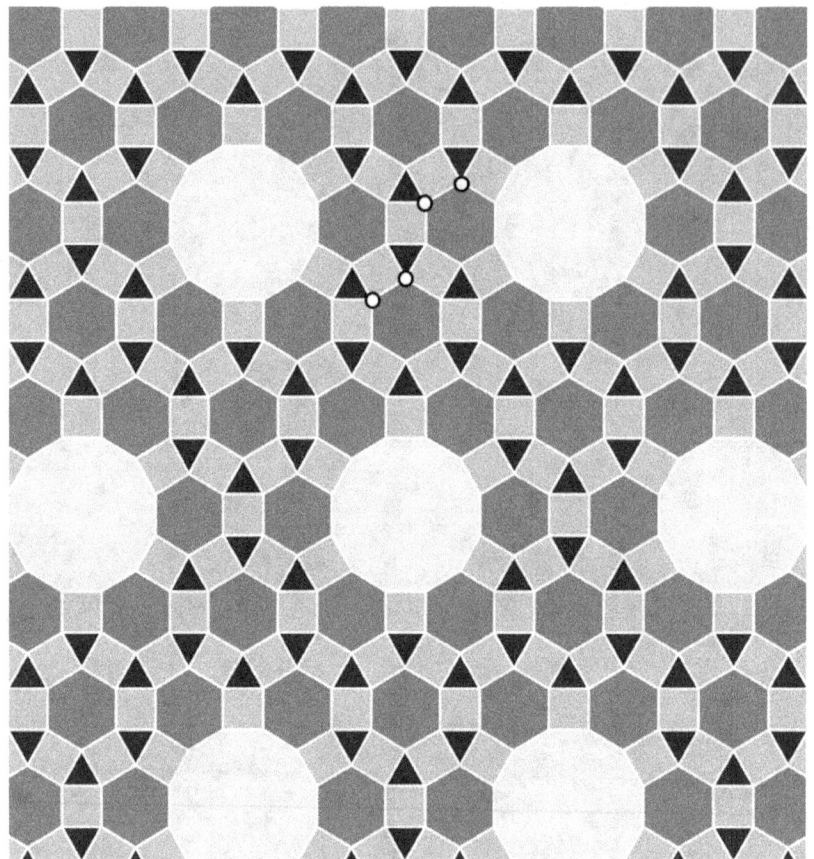

Figure 12. Example of a 5-uniform tessellation with only 2 vertex types

3.3   Convex Polygons

Thus far, we have only considered tessellations using regular polygons. It is also possible to tile the plane using convex polygons with sides of different length or angles of different measures.

Definition of a **convex polygon**: A polygon is convex if for any two points within or on the boundary of the polygon, it is possible to draw a line between the points such that the line is completely contained within the polygon, see Figure 13.

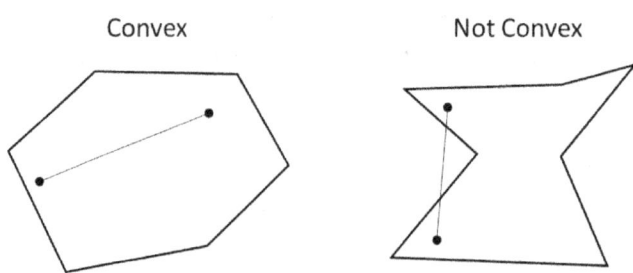

Figure 13. Convexity

As it turns out, the problem of tiling the plane with convex polygons is most interesting in the case of pentagons. In fact, the identification of all types of pentagons that can be used to tile the plane was only solved recently (and at that, some elements of the proof still need to be checked). Before we get to the details of convex pentagon tiling, we cover the simpler cases.

It is not possible to tile the plane with convex polygons having 7 or more sides. An intuitive proof of this fact can be found in the paper by Fischer [13]. A more rigorous proof is noted in Statement 9.1.1 of the book by Grunbaum and Shephard [14]. This leaves us to consider triangles (all of which are convex), quadrilaterals, pentagons and hexagons.

The case for triangles is easy, i.e., take any triangle, rotate it 180 degrees to form another triangle, put the two together to form a parallelogram which is then used to tile the plane. Going from left to right, Figure 14 shows the approach for isosceles, acute and obtuse triangles.

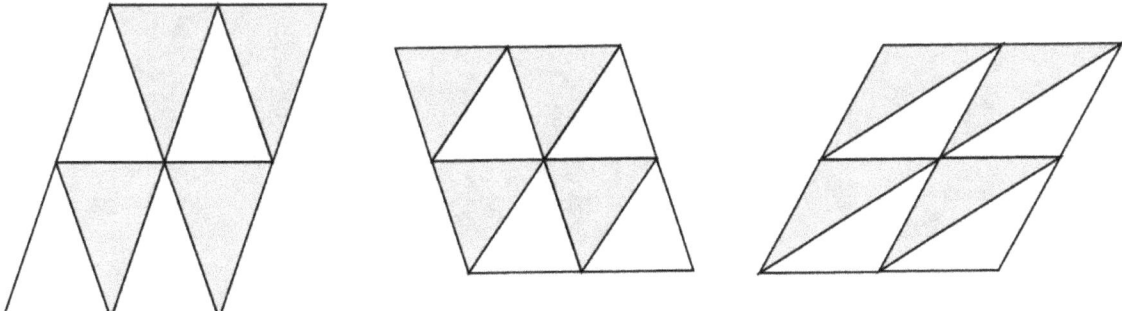

Figure 14. Tiling the plane with triangles

A very similar procedure works for quadrilaterals, whether they are convex or not. Take any quadrilateral, rotate it 180 degrees, put the two quadrilaterals together to form a hexagon. By construction, each edge of the hexagon is equal and parallel to its opposite edge. The hexagons can then be used to tile the plane. Figure 15 depicts examples for the convex and non-convex cases.

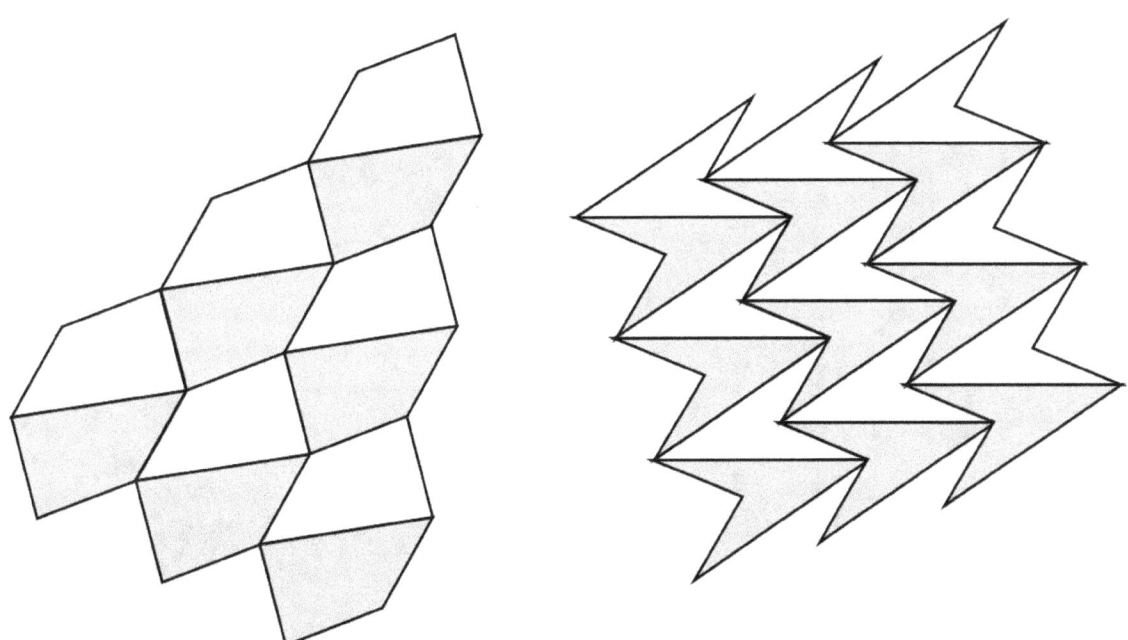

Figure 15. Tiling the plane with quadrilaterals

There are three types of convex hexagonal tilings of the plane. This fact was proven in 1918 by K. Reinhardt in his doctoral thesis at the University of Frankfurt. Each type of hexagonal tiling is described by conditions on the interior angles and sides of the tiling hexagon. Examples of the three types and associated conditions are shown in Figure 16, Figure 17 and Figure 18. Since only one type of hexagon is used to tiling the plane, these tilings are called monohedral convex hexagonal tilings. Other types of hexagonal tilings (as well as the monohedral types) are discussed in the Wikipedia article entitled "Hexagonal tiling" [15].

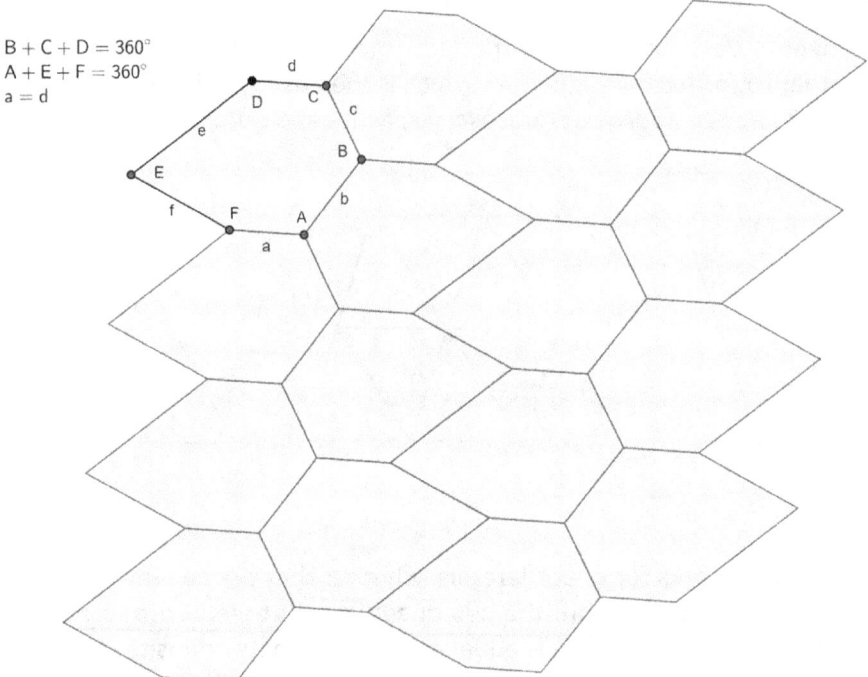

Figure 16. Type 1 convex hexagon tiling

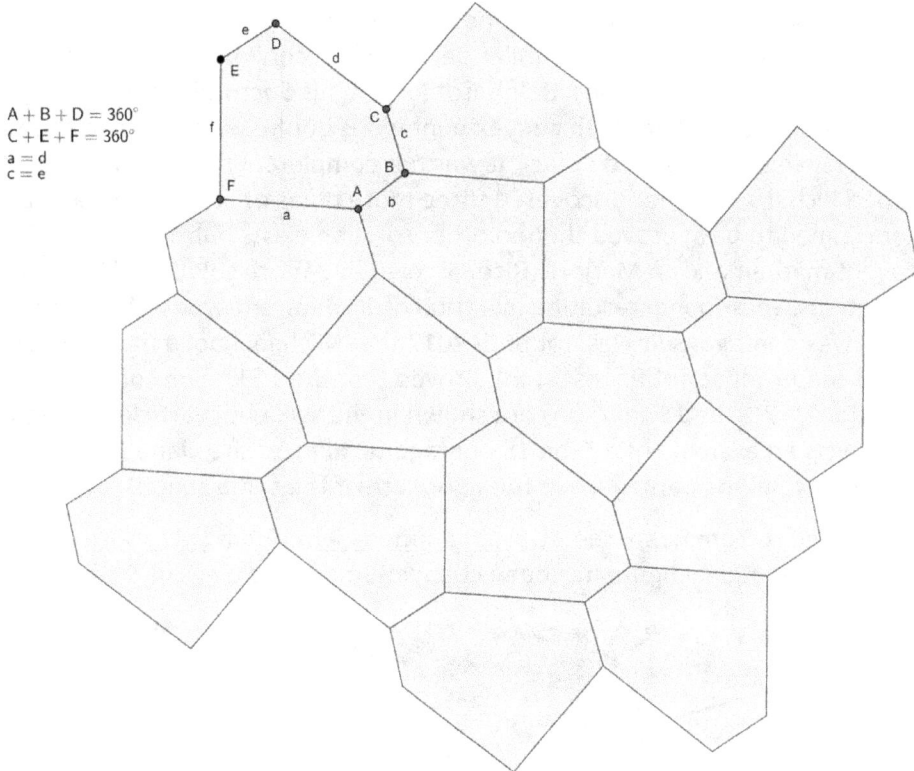

Figure 17. Type 2 convex hexagon tiling

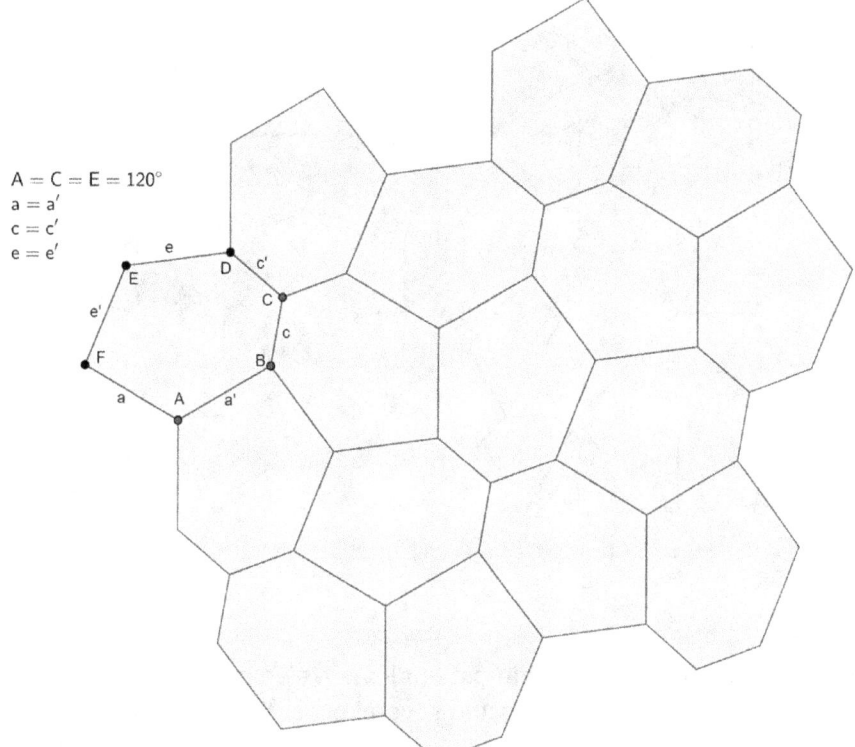

Figure 18. Type 3 convex hexagon tiling

The solution of the problem concerning a monohedral tiling of the plane with convex pentagons turned out to be very hard to solve. Using similar descriptive techniques to his identification of the monohedral tilings with convex hexagons, Reinhardt (also in his doctoral thesis) identified 5 different types of monohedral tilings with convex pentagons but he did not prove this was the complete set of possible solutions, and in fact, it was not complete. Progress on the problem stalled until in 1968 when Richard Kershner discovered three more types of convex pentagons that tile the plane. Kershner claimed to have proved that no other solution exists but his proof was not to stand. In 1975, self-taught mathematician Marjorie Rice discovered 3 more solutions [16]. Subsequently, several more solutions were found, resulting in a total of 15 different types of monohedral tilings of the plane with convex pentagons. It was not until 2017 that Michaël Rao, a mathematician at CNRS (France's national center for scientific research), proved that the 15 known solutions were the entire set of solutions [17]. The 15 solutions are shown in the Wikipedia article on pentagonal tiling [18]. Figure 19 depicts an example of a Type 15 pentagonal tiling of the plane (the shading is for visual effect and in fact, all the pentagons in the figure are of the same shape).

Credits for Figure 19 go to Tom Ruen, see https://commons.wikimedia.org/wiki/File:P5-type15-chiral_coloring.png. The original figure has been changed to grayscale.

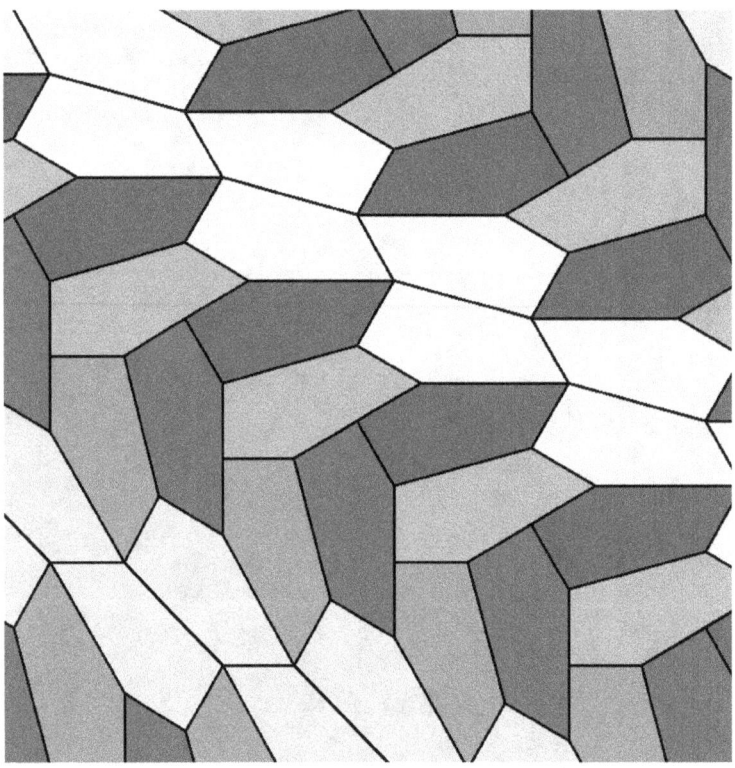

Figure 19. Example of a Type 15 convex pentagonal tiling

3.4   Other Types of Tessellations

The variations regarding tessellations are almost endless. We've only covered a few of the more common types. In this section, we briefly discuss several other types of tessellations.

3.4.1   Non-periodic Tessellations

All the tessellations that we have seen so far are periodic in the sense that one can make a copy of the tessellation, translate the copy to another position in the plane, and then drop the copy on top of the original and get an exact match. If this is not possible, then the tessellation is classified as **non-periodic** (also known as aperiodic). Non-periodic tilings are said to lack translation symmetry. The definitions of periodic and non-periodic apply to any type of tiling (not just those involving polygons).

Figure 20 is a very simple but uninteresting example of a non-periodic tiling. The two triangles (which repeat nowhere else) disrupt the periodicity of the tiling.

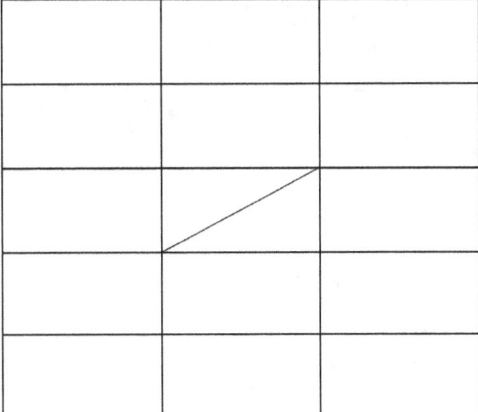

Figure 20. Simple non-periodic tiling

A complex example is the rhomb tiling in Figure 21. The source for Figure 21 and the details for constructing similar figures can be found in the online article by Tjipke Hibma [20], see the figure entitled "Quarter-rhomb tiling for n=11." Unlike the figures for periodic tilings, the rhomb tiling figure itself does not provide sufficient information to continue the pattern. The figure looks very ordered, and one might think (without detailed observation) that the rhomb tiling is periodic, but it is not.

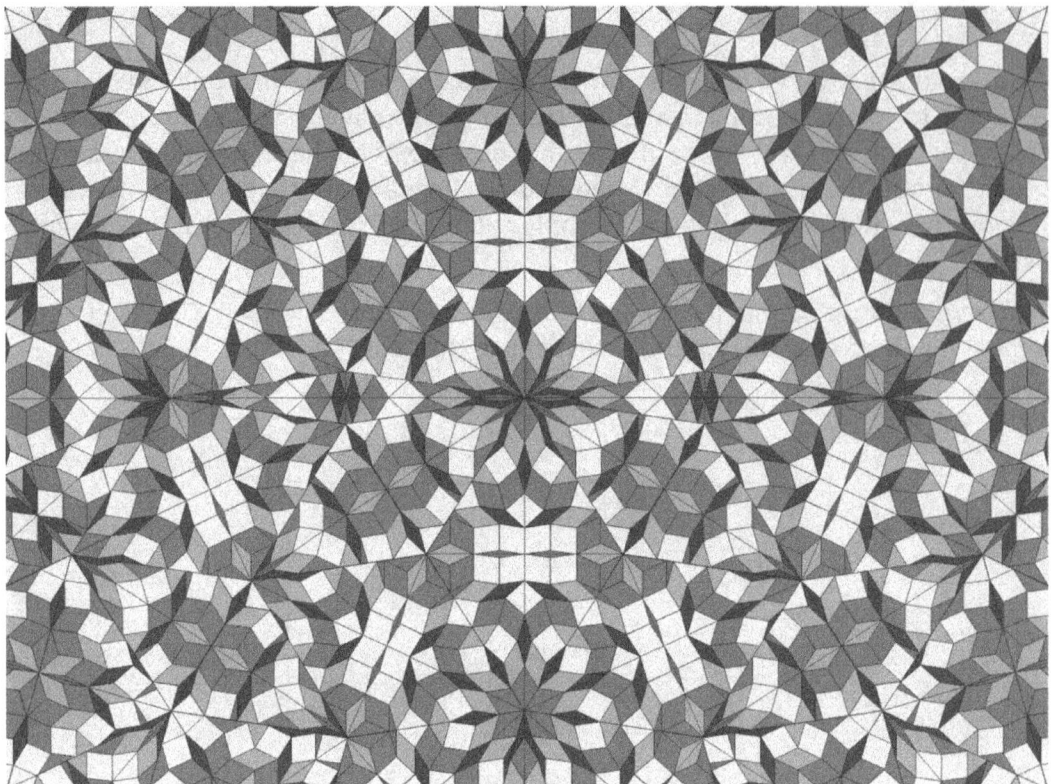

Figure 21. Example of a rhomb tiling

Perhaps the most famous non-periodic tiling is the eponymous Penrose tiling [21]. While the Penrose tilings lack translational symmetry, it does have reflection symmetry and five-fold rotational symmetry. An example Penrose tiling is shown in Figure 22. (Note that "P3" in the title of the figure refers to one of three types of Penrose tilings, and yes, the other two types are called P1 and P2.)

The following YouTube videos cover various aspects of periodic and non-periodic tilings.

- A two-part series on fundamentals of periodic (https://youtu.be/yKyZlK1Ch0M) and aperiodic (https://youtu.be/hraRYYPjtCk) tilings

- Penrose tiles: *Helsinki Maths Mystery* at https://youtu.be/yxlEojkVJ0c and the video entitled *The Penrose Tessellation* at http://penrose.dmf.unicatt.it/html5_penrose.html.en

- Roger Penrose - Forbidden crystal symmetry in mathematics and architecture: https://youtu.be/th3YMEamzmw (this is a lecture from Roger Penrose).

Also, see the online book entitled "Math and the Art of MC Escher" [19] which has a section on aperiodic tessellations as well as several other sections on different aspects of tessellations.

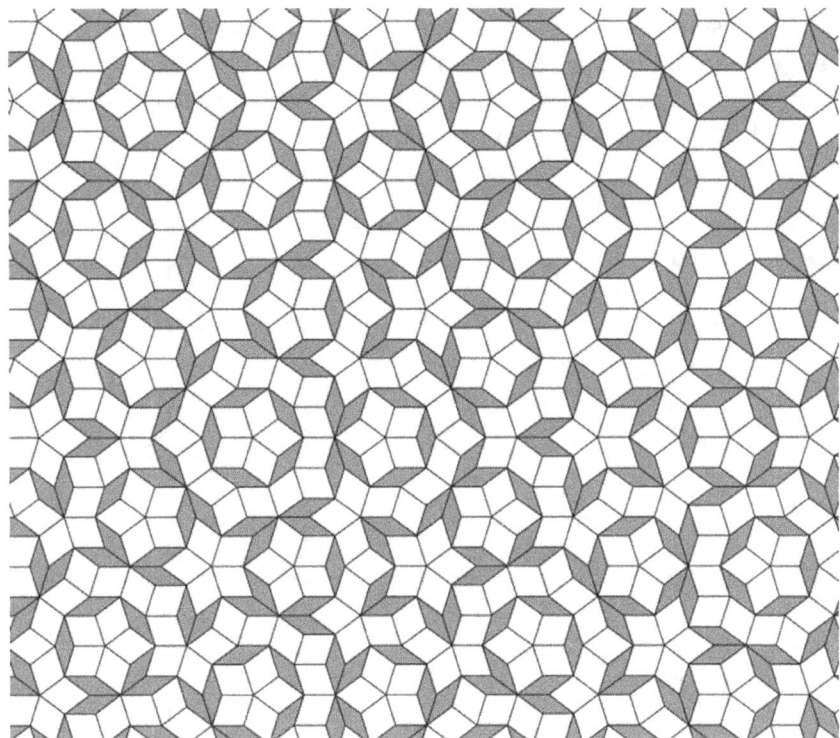

Figure 22. Example of a Penrose P3 tiling

3.4.2   Wallpaper Groups

Wallpaper groups are a mathematical concept used to classify repeating patterns that are often used in architecture, decorative art (e.g., textiles and tiles) and of course, wallpaper.

Figure 23 shows an example of a simple wallpaper design comprised of icons for an ambulance. Each ambulance is a units away horizontally and b units away vertically from the next closest ambulance. If the pattern is moved any combination of $\pm a$ units horizontally and $\pm b$ units vertically, we get the same pattern. This property is known as translation symmetry. The asymmetry of the ambulance icon prevents this wallpaper from having any other symmetries.

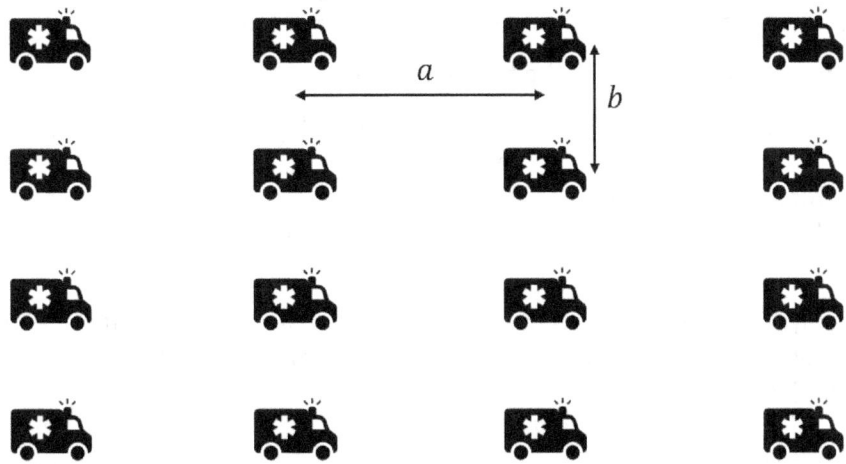

Figure 23. Wallpaper with translation symmetry

In addition to translation symmetry, the wallpaper in Figure 24 has reflection symmetry. If the pattern is reflected (flipped) along any of the dashed lines (referred to as axes of reflection), we get the same pattern. Any type of rotational symmetry is prevented by the asymmetry of the airplane icon (e.g., the top and bottom of each airplane is different).

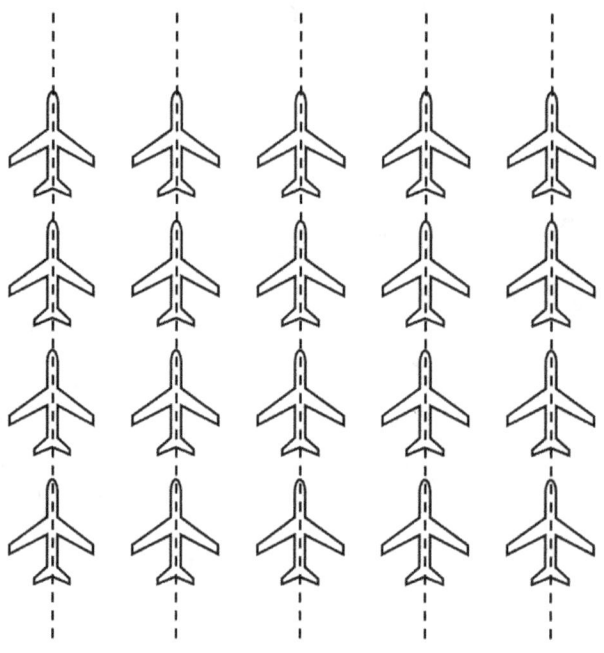

Figure 24. Wallpaper with reflection symmetry

The wallpaper pattern in Figure 25 has translation symmetry and extensive reflection symmetries (the axes of reflection are shown as dashed lines). Unlike the previous two examples, the wallpaper pattern in Figure 25 has rotational symmetries:

- There is a 90 degrees (4-fold) rotation symmetry at each of the points where three of the axes of reflection intersect (one example is marked by a triangle in the figure) and also from the center of each circle.

- There is a 180 degrees (2-fold) rotational symmetry at each of the points where only two of the axes of reflection intersect (one example is marked by a star in the figure).

(Neither the dashed lines, the star nor the triangle are part of the pattern.)

It turns out that 2-fold (180 degrees), 3-fold (120 degrees), 4-fold (90 degrees) and 6-fold (60 degrees) are the only possible rotational symmetries for wallpaper groups. This result is known as the Crystallographic Restriction Theorem [22]. The crystallographic restriction theorem is based on the observation that the rotational symmetries of a crystal are usually limited to 2-fold, 3-fold, 4-fold, and 6-fold.

As stated previously, the Penrose tilings have 5-fold rotational symmetry but the Penrose tilings do not meet the condition of a repeating pattern which is assumed for wallpaper groups.

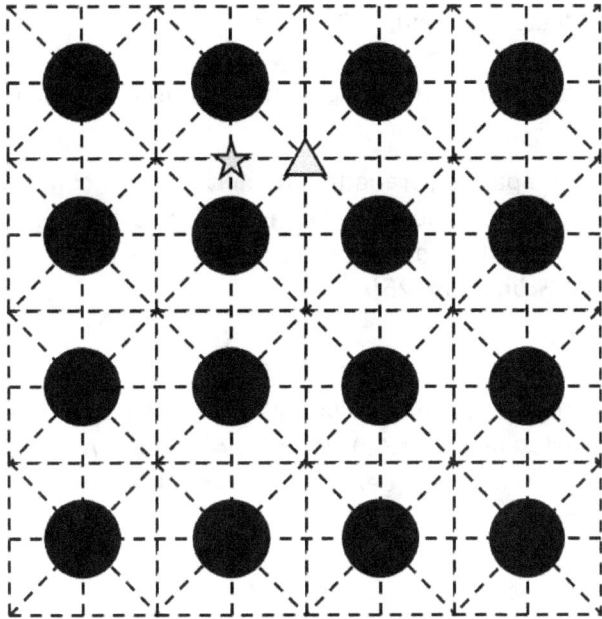

Figure 25. Wallpaper with rotational symmetry

The pattern in Figure 26 exhibits the fourth type of symmetric (i.e., glide-reflection) that can be realized in a wallpaper design. A glide-reflection entails a reflection about an axis and then a translation along that same axis. The solid lines in the figure are two examples of the infinite number of glide-reflections in the pattern. Consider the vertical solid line. If we reflect the pattern about that line, the pattern is out of phase. However, if after the flip we move the pattern up (or down) one unit (length between the center of the circles), then the pattern is aligned again. The pattern in Figure 26 also has an infinite number of reflections (see the two examples shown as dashed-lines). Further, it should be noted that all reflections can be considered as glide-reflections where the glide is just 0 movement.

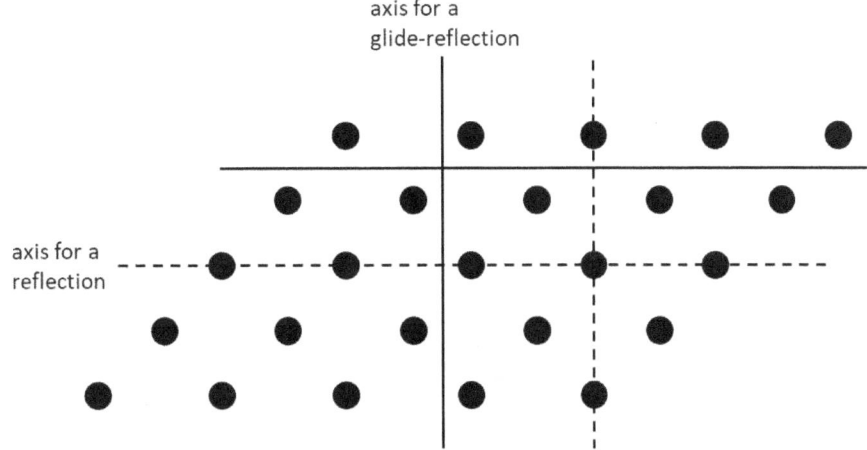

Figure 26. Wallpaper with glide-reflection symmetry

Using various combinations of translation, reflection, rotation and glide-reflection symmetries, it can be shown that there are exactly 17 different types of wallpaper groups. This fact was first proven by Evgraf Fedorov in 1891 and then derived independently by George Pólya in 1924. The

Wikipedia article entitled "Wallpaper group" [23] describes and proves an example of each type of wallpaper group. See also the website at http://clowder.net/hop/17walppr/17walppr.html which gives an example of each wallpaper group along with animations for each type of symmetry pertaining to a given group.

The tilings within the Alhambra palace (Granada, Andalusia, Spain) contain many of the wallpaper groups (see the photos at "Tile Decoration Alhambra Palace Spain Stock Photos" [24]). However, there is some debate as to exactly how many of the patterns are represented in the Alhambra, see the journal article by Branko Grünbaum [25].

3.4.3   Free-style Tessellations

This section covers what I call "free-style tessellations." The idea is to create variations of known structured tessellations. Artists, such as M.C. Escher, have created numerous tilings based on creative variations of the basic tilings. The general idea is to alter the edges of the tiles and to draw recognizable figures in the interior of the tiles. See the online galleries at https://mcescher.com/gallery/symmetry/ and http://www.tessellations.org/eschergallery2thumbs.shtml for a collection of M.C. Escher tessellations. If you look closely, you can see the faint lines for the underlying geometric shapes used as a basis for each drawing.

As an example construction (sadly much less creative than Escher), consider a rectangle and make some changes, as shown in Figure 27.

- First, replace the left-side of the rectangle with a curved shape (with no loops). Make the same replacement on the left-side of the rectangle. These changes ensure that the right and left sides of the modified rectangles fit together.

- Next, replace the bottom-side of the rectangle with another curved shape (with no loops) and make the same replacement on the top-side of the rectangle. This ensures that the top and bottom of the modified rectangles fit together.

- Remove the rectangle, leaving the tile at the bottom of Figure 27.

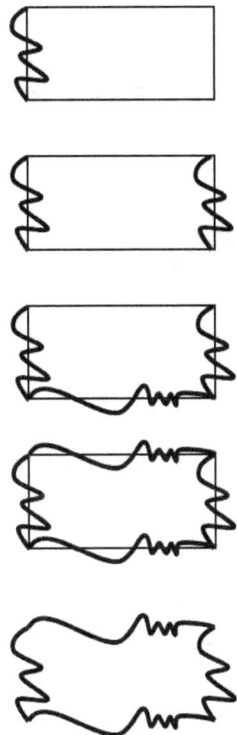

Figure 27. Steps in Creation a Rectangle-based Tessellation

The tile from Figure 27 can be used to create a tiling of the plane, as shown in Figure 28. The pattern has translation symmetry but no other symmetry.

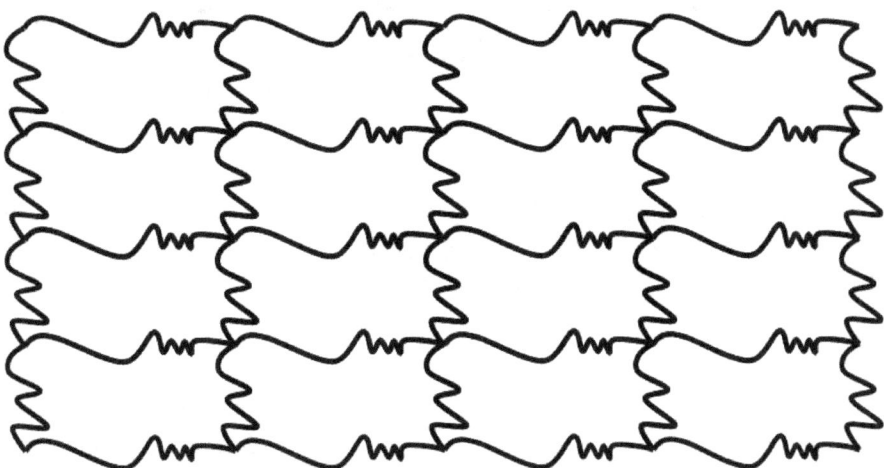

Figure 28. Rectangle-based Tessellation

The same idea can be used on other shapes. The tile in Figure 29 is based on a parallelogram.

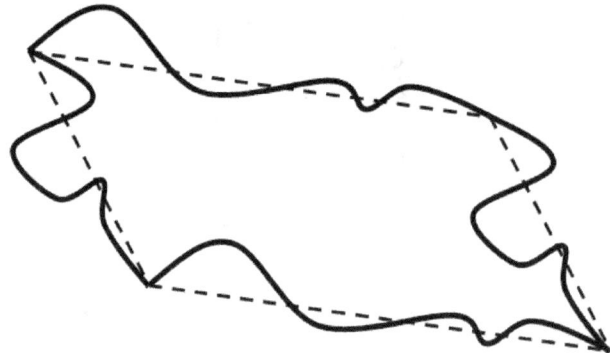

Figure 29. Repeating Element for Parallelogram-based Tessellation

The tile in Figure 29 is used to tile the plane with the pattern shown in Figure 30. Again, the only symmetry is that of translation.

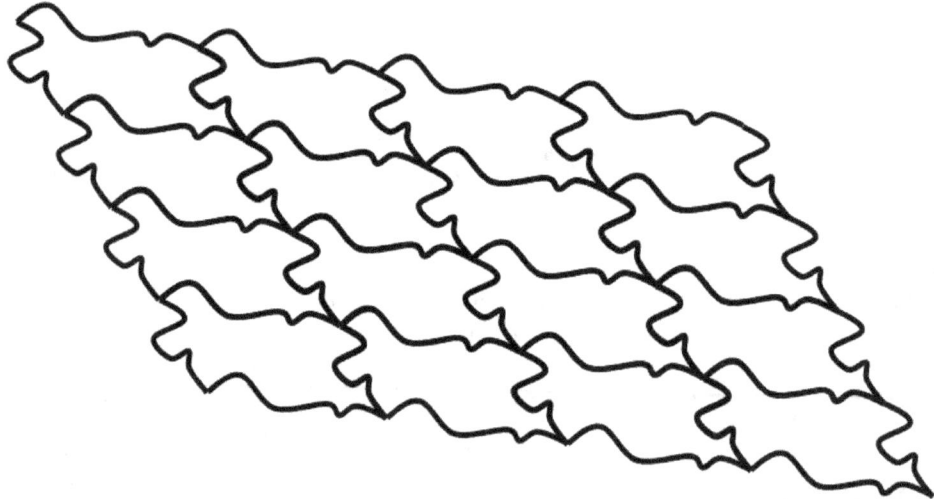

Figure 30. Parallelogram-based Tessellation

It is possible to use other base shapes (such triangles and hexagrams) to create tiles that tessellate the plane. For further details on how to create such drawings, see the section entitled "Tessellations by Recognizable Figures" in the online book "Math and the Art of MC Escher" [19].

3.4.4   Isohedral Tilings

Digging a bit deeper into the tilings from the previous section, many of the "free-style tessellations" by M.C. Escher and others can be classified as isohedral tilings. Escher created dozens of different shapes which fit together in various ways to produce isohedral tilings.

3.4.4.1   Definition

Isohedral tilings are a subset of the set of monohedral tilings. Monohedral tilings consist of one type of tile and allow for non-periodic patterns, e.g., see the spiral monohedral tiling in Figure 31. This tiling was discovered by Heinz Voderberg in 1936 and is considered to be the first spiral monohedral tiling. To be clear, the Voderberg tiling is an example of a monohedral tiling which is **not** an isohedral tiling.

Figure credits to TED-43, see https://commons.wikimedia.org/wiki/File:Voderberg-1.png. The original figure was changed to grayscale.

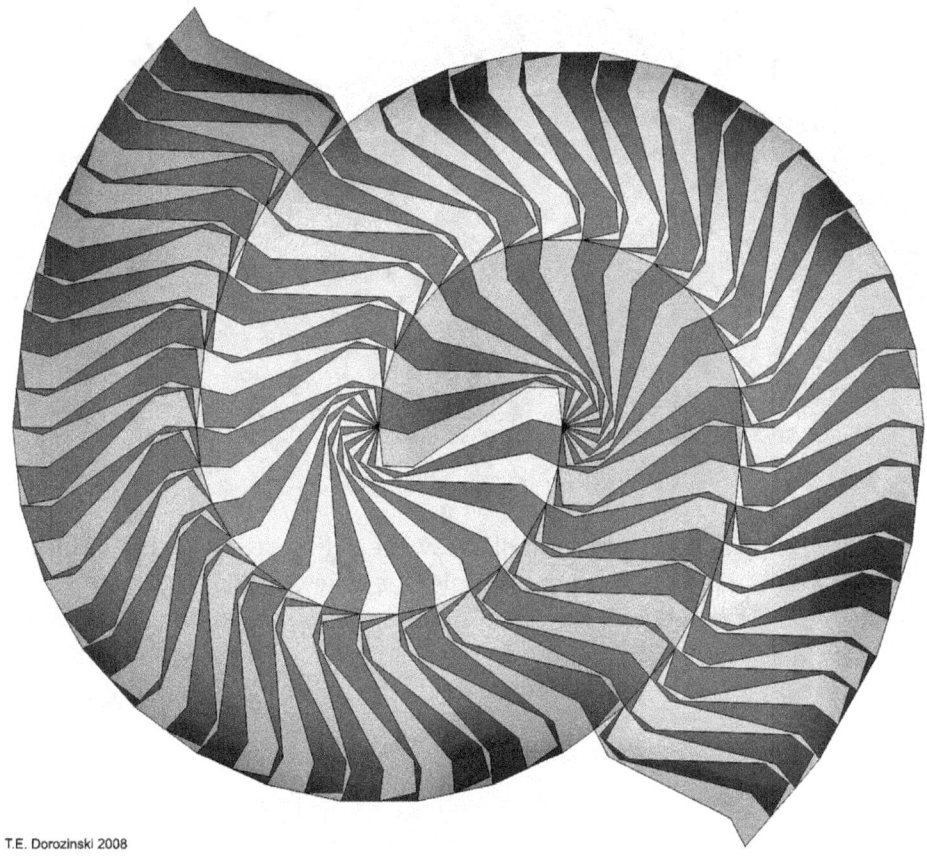

T.E. Dorozinski 2008

Figure 31. Voderberg tiling

The definition of an **isohedral tiling** is a bit intricate. In her book "Geometric symmetry in patterns and tilings" [26], Clare E. Horne offers several wordings of essentially the same definition:

> If each tile can be mapped onto any other tile by a symmetry of the tiling, then the tiling is isohedral. Lenart [27] defines an isohedral tiling more simply by saying that a monohedral tiling T is called isohedral if, given two tiles t_i and t_j, there is a symmetry transformation of the entire tiling which maps t_i onto t_j.

> Again, the simplest way to assess whether a translational tiling is isohedral is to look at a translation unit. If, inside one translation unit, each tile can be mapped onto any other by an isometry of the tiling, then by subsequent unit translations, any tile can be mapped onto any other in the whole tiling.

Figure 32 depicts a simple herringbone brick pattern of a pavement. The pattern is an isohedral tiling since any brick (tile) can be transformed to any other brick while preserving the pattern. This is done either by a translation (vertical or horizontal motion), reflection or glide-reflection.

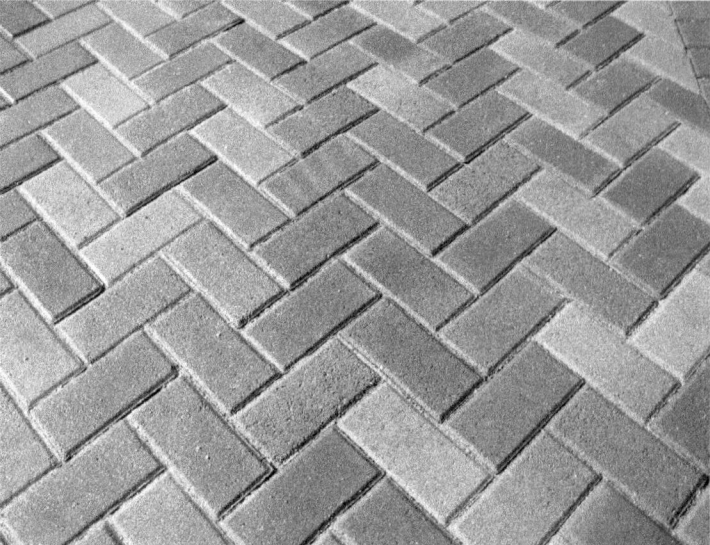

Figure 32. Herringbone Brick Pattern

Both of the tile patterns in Figure 33 are periodic. However, the pattern on the left is an isohedral tiling and the pattern on the right is not. For example, the gray tile in the pattern on the left can be mapped to the black tile via reflection of the entire pattern about a horizontal axis and then a translation, as shown in Figure 34. On the other hand, there is no transformation that takes the gray tile in the pattern on the right to the black tile. So, the pattern on the right is not isohedral.

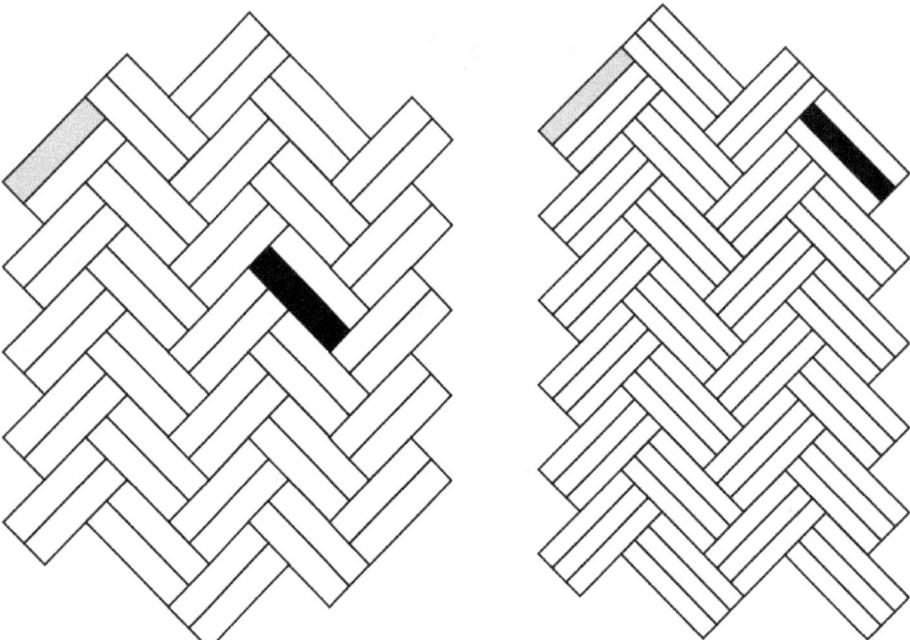

Figure 33. Brick patterns

The left-side of Figure 34 shows the original pattern (from the left-side of Figure 33), the reflection of the original pattern, and how the reflection is to be placed over the original. The right-side of the figure shows the reflection as placed over the original pattern. This can be done for any two tiles in the pattern and so the pattern is isohedral.

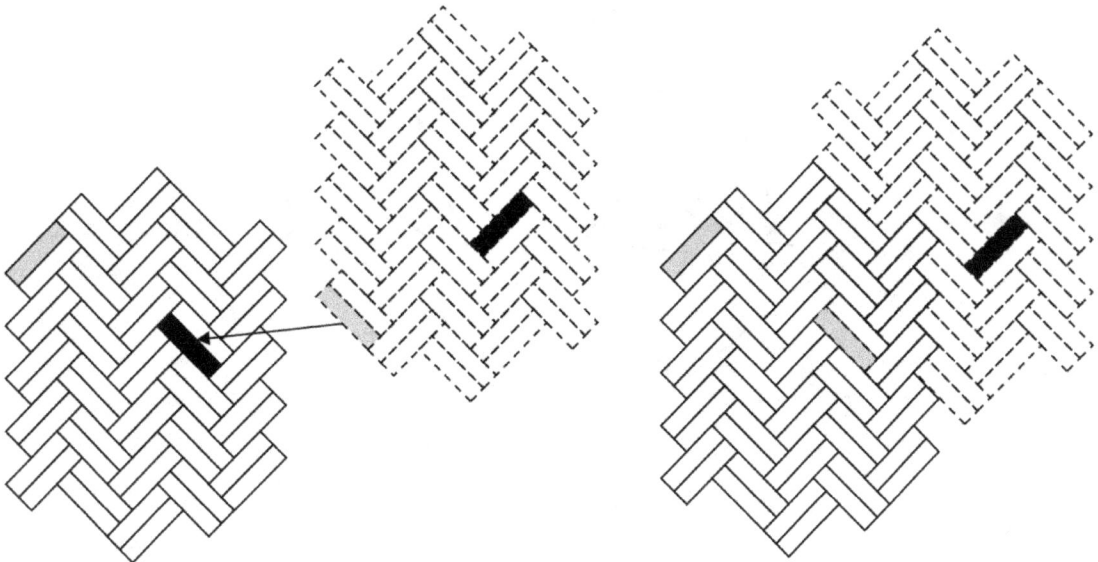

Figure 34. Transformation of One Brick to Another

3.4.4.2 Classification

The set of isohedral tiling types has been completely classified. This was first done by Branko Grunbaum and G.C. Shephard in Tilings and Patterns [14] (see Chapter 6, "Classification of Tilings with Transitivity Properties). There are a total of 93 isohedral mappings which are labeled from IH1 to IH93. The naming scheme is from Grunbaum and Shephard where presumably IH is an abbreviation for IsoHedral.

In addition to the mathematical understanding of such patterns, the classification is also useful to artists who can select various patterns and then add their artistic elements.

The explanation of the classification scheme from Grunbaum and Shephard is a bit technical (using a branch of mathematics known as group theory). In the explanation that follows, we make use of the more accessible approach by McLean [28]. To be clear, McLean describes the same classification as Grunbaum and Shephard, it is just the nomenclature that differs.

An example of the general approach taken by McLean is as follows. First, start with a specific example of an isohedral tiling. We will use the pattern in Figure 35. The drawings inside some of the tiles are just for decoration and do not affect the analysis that follows.

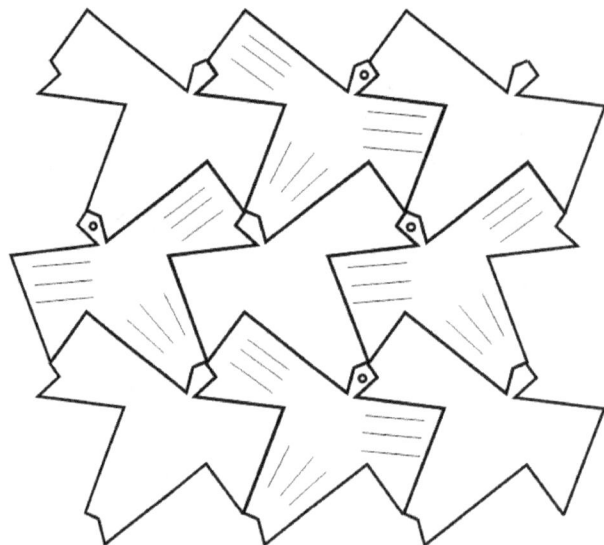

Figure 35. Abstract bird pattern based on a parallelogram

The next step is to identify the points on a given tile where three or more tiles meet. For the problem at hand, there are 4 points on each tile where a total of three tiles meet (see points a, b, c and d in tile on the left of Figure 36). From here, we identify the general characteristic of the pattern:

- Sides ab and dc have the same pattern but reflected about a vertical axis. This is represented by the two white triangles pointing in opposite directions (middle item in figure).

- Sides ad and bc have the exact same pattern. This is represented by the two black arrows pointing in the same direction.

- There is no rotation or reflection symmetry in the pattern. This is denoted by the F in the middle of the template. The letter "F" is used since it has no rotation or reflection symmetry.

At this point, we have identified the pattern for a particular isohedral tiling (IH43 to use the naming scheme from Grunbaum and Shephard). The left-side of Figure 36 illustrates how multiple copies of the template can be tiled together. The key point here is that we now have a general pattern. As long as the conditions in the three bullet items above are followed, one can use many different images (with the "abstract bird" being just one example).

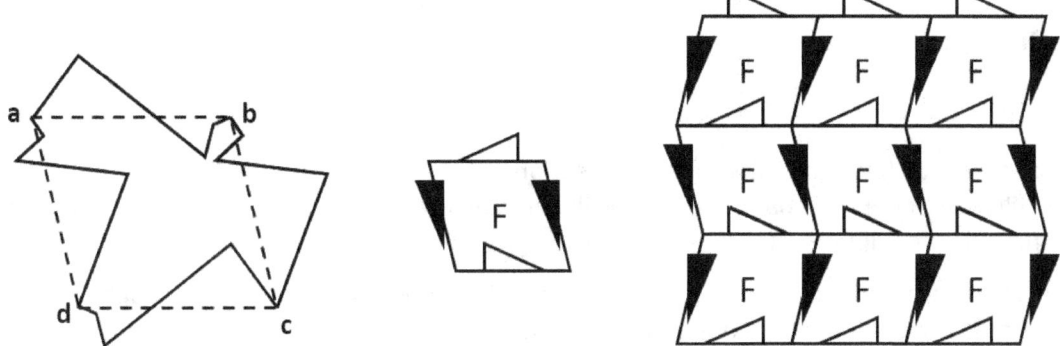

Figure 36. Template associated with abstract bird pattern

As additional examples, note that the patterns in Figure 28 and Figure 30 both obey the conditions of isohedral pattern IH41 (shown in Figure 37), i.e., opposite sides are equal and there is no internal rotation of reflection symmetries.

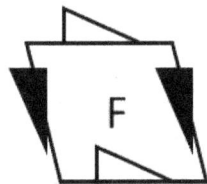

Figure 37. Isohedral pattern IH41

The herringbone brick pattern in Figure 32 is a bit harder to classify. As can be seen from Figure 38, each brick has 6 points where 3 or more vertices meet. This means the pattern is of the hexagonal type (albeit a flatten hexagon). The internal angles of the hexagon are 180 degrees at points a and d, and 90 degrees at the other four angles. Each brick has horizontal and vertical reflection symmetry as well as 180 degree reflection symmetry. All the sides are equal. This means that the herringbone pattern satisfies the conditions of IH9, IH14 and IH17, and adds some conditions. See specific examples of IH9, IH14 and IH17 at https://www.jaapsch.net/tilings/mclean/html/ih17.html and https://www.jaapsch.net/tilings/mclean/html/ih9.html, respectively.

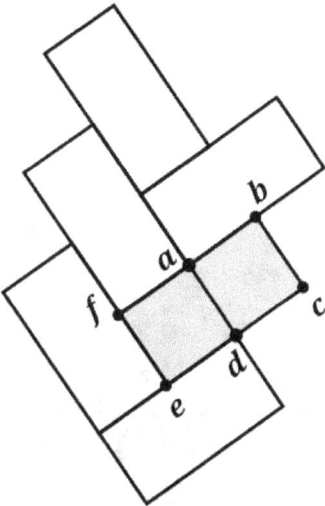

Figure 38. Analysis of herringbone brick pattern

4   Perspective

4.1   Overview

Linear perspective (also known as point-projection perspective) is a technique used by artists to give the illusion of depth in paintings. The Wikipedia article entitled "Perspective (graphical)" [29] offers the following definition:

> Linear or point-projection perspective (from Latin: perspicere 'to see through') is one of two types of graphical projection perspective in the graphic arts; the other is parallel projection. Linear perspective is an approximate representation, generally on a flat surface, of an image as it is seen by the eye. The most characteristic features of linear perspective are that objects appear smaller as their distance from the observer increases, and that they are subject to foreshortening, meaning that an object's dimensions along the line of sight appear shorter than its dimensions across the line of sight. All objects will recede to points in the distance, usually along the horizon line, but also above and below the horizon line depending on the view used.

In photographic art, perspective comes almost automatically. For example, Figure 39 is a photograph (taken in Nice, France by the author of this book) that illustrates single-point perspective. Notice how the buildings on the left and the scenery on the right get smaller as they approach the vanishing point in the middle of the photo (where the arrow is pointing). The reflecting pool in the center of the photo is actually rectangular but becomes narrower in the photo as one approaches the vanishing point. [From the Merriam-Webster dictionary: "**vanishing point** - a point at which receding parallel lines seem to meet when represented in linear perspective."]

One would think it natural for art to mimic photography when it comes to representing perspective but keep in mind that photography did not exist when artists first started to explore techniques for representing depth in artworks.

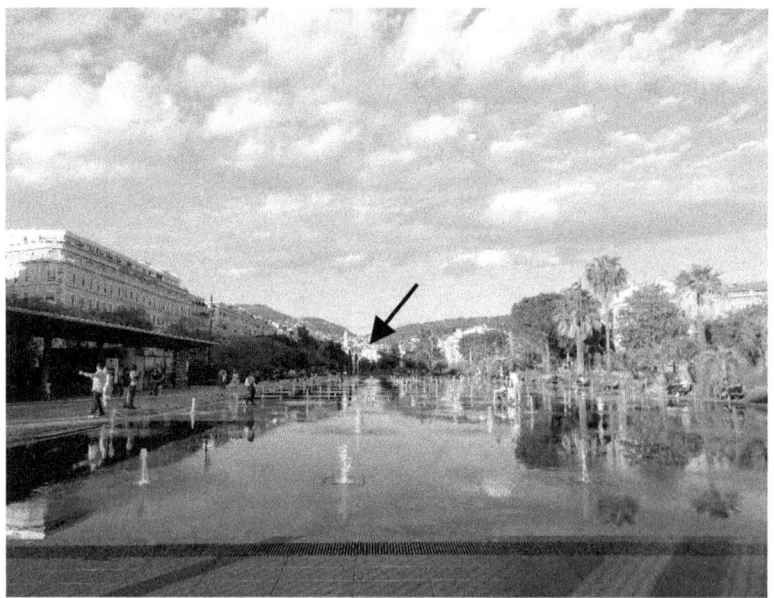

Figure 39. Photograph exhibiting single-point perspective

The vanishing point does not need to be in the center of photo or painting. For example, the vanishing point in Figure 40 is at the center-left of the photo (as shown by the arrow). In fact, it is possible to have multiple vanishing points.

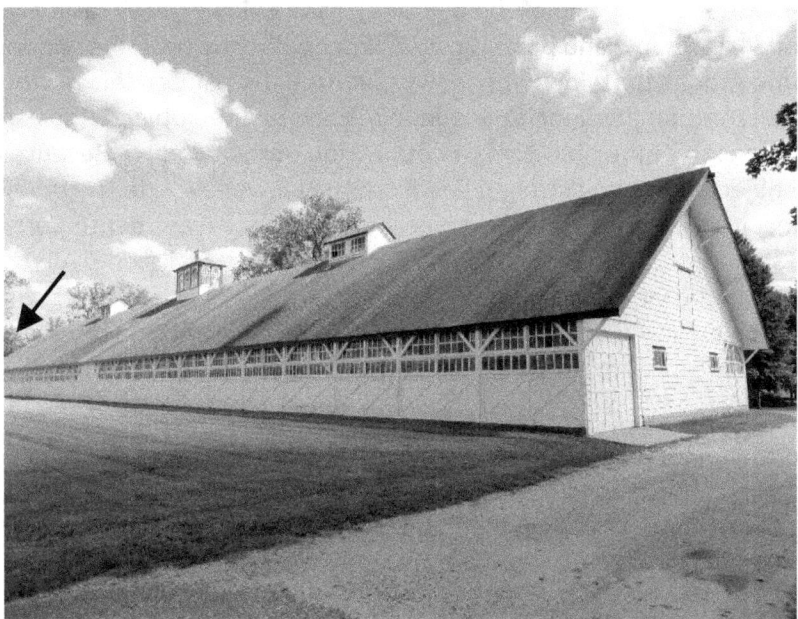

Figure 40. Vanishing point on the left

Figure 41 has an infinite number of vanishing points, i.e., the entire horizon where the ocean meets the sky.

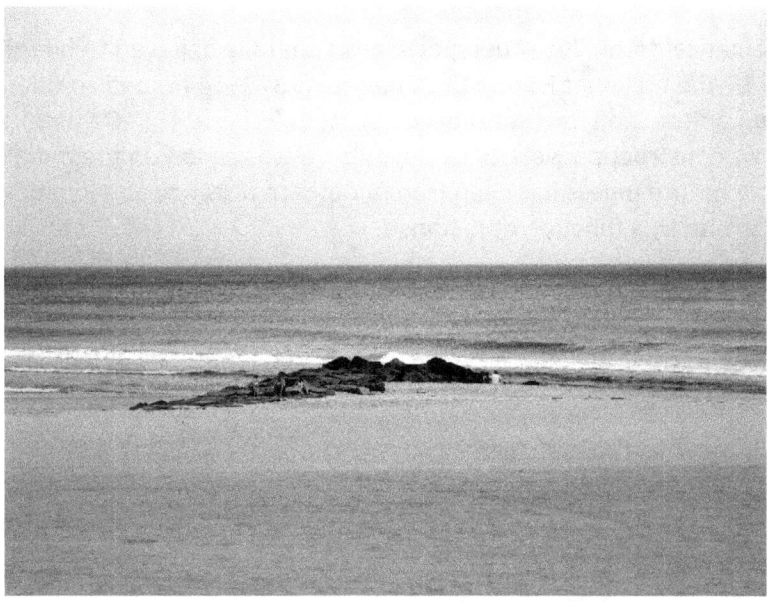

Figure 41. Infinite number of vanishing points

The task at hand (whether via photography or painting) is to realistically represent a 3-dimensional (3D) scene on a 2-dimensional (2D) surface. As noted, a camera does this automatically by capturing a 3-dimensional image on its 2-dimensional sensor. A low-tech approach is to trace a scene on a pane of glass. This approach is beautifully explained in the Wikipedia article on perspective [29]:

> Perspective works by representing the light that passes from a scene through an imaginary rectangle (realized as the plane of the painting), to the viewer's eye, as if a viewer were looking through a window and painting what is seen directly onto the windowpane. If viewed from the same spot as the windowpane was painted, the painted image would be identical to what was seen through the unpainted window. Each painted object in the scene is thus a flat, scaled down version of the object on the other side of the window. Because each portion of the painted object lies on the straight line from the viewer's eye to the equivalent portion of the real object it represents, the viewer sees no difference (sans depth perception) between the painted scene on the windowpane and the view of the real scene. All perspective drawings assume the viewer is a certain distance away from the drawing. Objects are scaled relative to that viewer. An object is often not scaled evenly: a circle often appears as an ellipse and a square can appear as a trapezoid. This distortion is referred to as **foreshortening**.

It should be noted that perspective is not the only technique used by artists to give depth to their drawings and paintings. Other techniques included overlapping, shading and shadowing, and the focus effect. For a detailed discussion on techniques used to give 2-dimensional art the appearance of three dimensions, see the book by D'Amelio and Hohauser [30].

4.2 Brief History

The use of perspective in art dates back to the 5th century BC (see the Section entitled Early History in the Wikipedia article on perspective [29]). However, it was not until the Renaissance that a mathematical theory of perspective was developed, as noted in the article The History of Perspective [31]:

> In its mathematical form, linear perspective is generally believed to have been devised about 1415 by the architect Filippo Brunelleschi (1377–1446) and codified in writing by the architect and writer Leon Battista Alberti (1404–1472), in 1435 (De pictura, i.e., On Painting). The construction worked out by Alberti was based on the belief that no picture can resemble nature unless it is seen from a definite distance and location, and the diminution in size as a function of distance.

The initial focus, and for several centuries thereafter, was on single-point perspective (i.e., a single vanishing point). Figure 42 is a painting by Saenredam which clearly makes use of a single vanishing point. The lines have been superimposed to illustrate the concept. The single vanishing point is at the intersection of the lines.

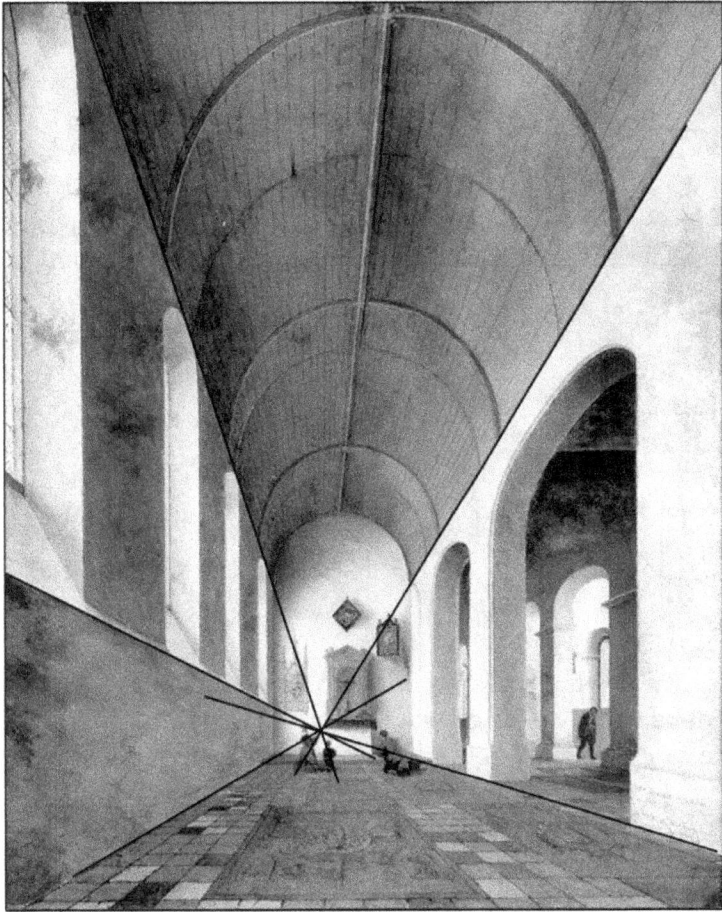

Figure 42. "St. Antoniuskapel in the St. Janskerk at Utrecht" by Pieter Jansz. Saenredam (1645)

From the article The History of Perspective [31]:

> For almost four hundred years after 1500, one-point perspective served as the standard
> technique for any painter who wished to create a systematic illusion of receding forms on a
> flat surface, be it canvas, wall or ceiling, although in many cases, perspective remained one
> of many strands woven into pictures of the time.

4.3   Examples

In single-point perspective, there is a single vanishing point. All figures in a painting (or drawing) are
projected to the vanishing point. Figure 43 shows several cubes drawn using single-point
perspective. Three cases are depicted, i.e., cube above the horizon containing the vanishing point,
below the horizon and at the horizon. Notice how the edges on the side of each cube angle towards
the vanishing point. This type of angling toward the vanishing point is also evident in the buildings
on the left of Figure 39.

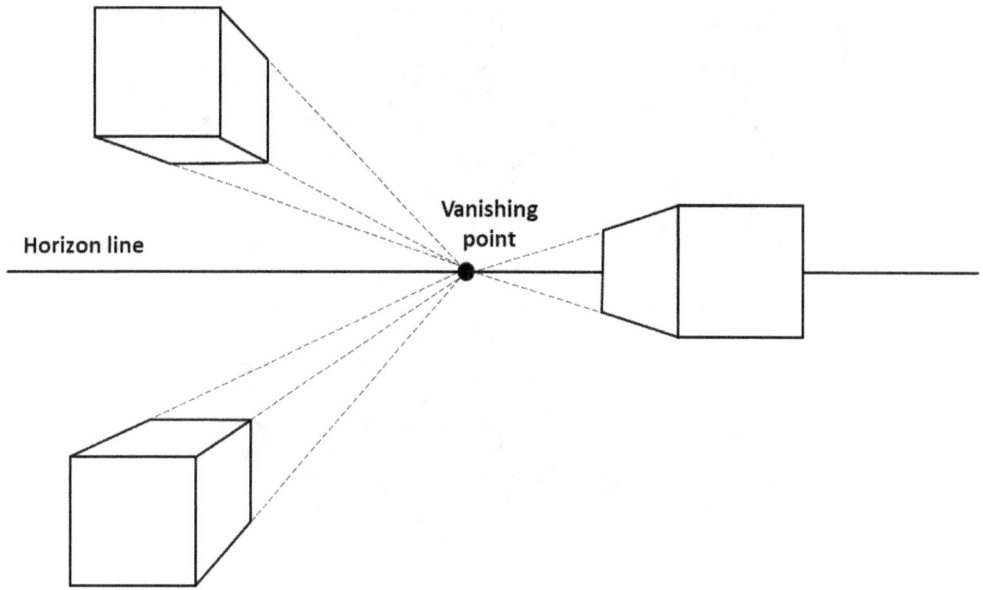

Figure 43. Example of single-point perspective

As the name suggests, two-point perspective entails a drawing with two vanishing points on the horizon line. Two-point perspective is used when an object is viewed from an edge rather than a face. For example, the block in Figure 44 is drawn in two-point perspective. An edge of the block is facing the viewer.

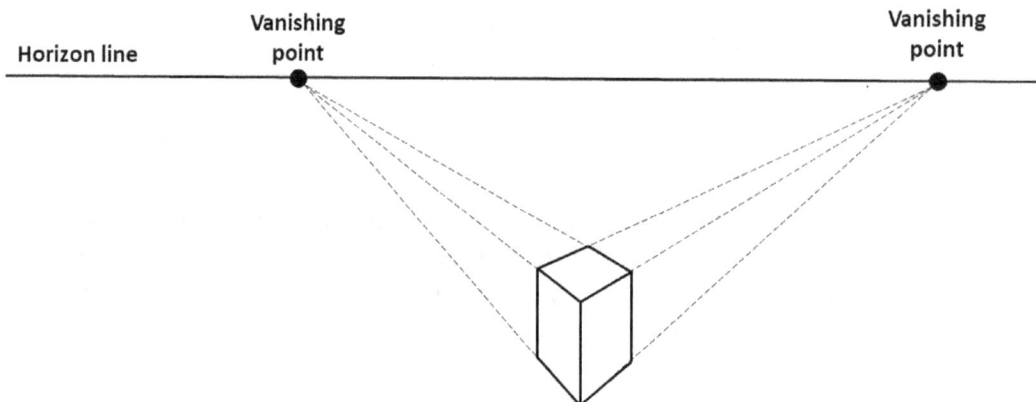

Figure 44. Example of two-point perspective

The Merriam-Webster dictionary gives the following definition of **two-point perspective**:

> Linear perspective in which parallel lines along the width and depth of an object are represented as meeting at two separate points on the horizon that are 90 degrees apart as measured from the common intersection of the lines of projection.

The condition about "90 degrees apart" can be relaxed (i.e., not followed). For example, the photo of the Flatiron building (New York city) in Figure 45 is taken from a two-point perspective but clearly, the two streets (5th Avenue and Broadway) are not at 90 degrees. The vanishing points (added to the photo) are the small white circles at the top of the photo. (Credits: the photo was taken from Google online maps.)

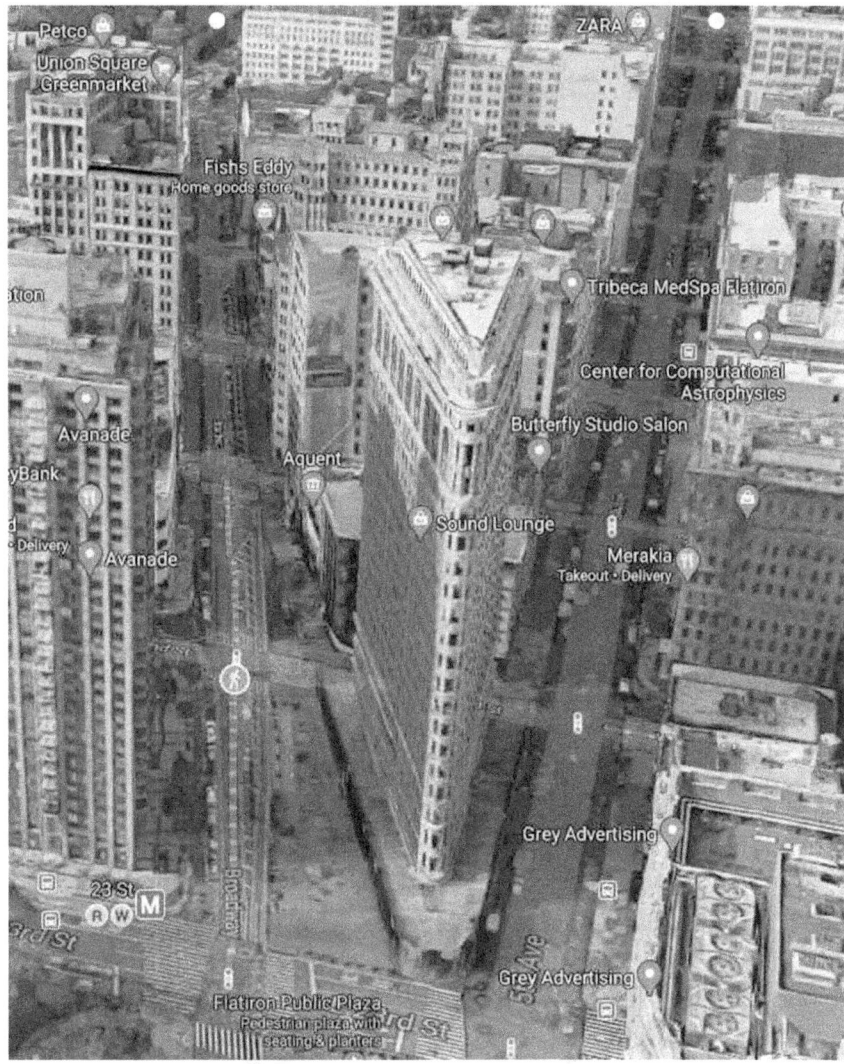

Figure 45. Flatiron building (New York City) from a two-point perspective

Figure 46, Figure 47 and Figure 48 illustrate the drawing of a simple room from a two-point perspective. In the first step (Figure 46), the back edge of the room (solid vertical line) and adjacent walls are drawn. Notice that the left wall is focused on the vanishing point on the right, and vice versa for the right wall.

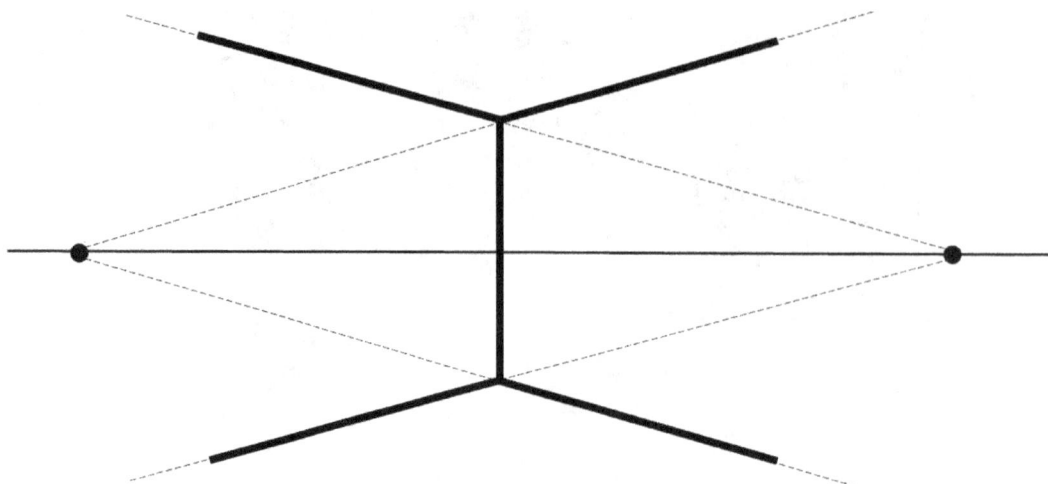

Figure 46. Drawing a room in two-point perspective – Step 1

In the second step (Figure 47), a window and bed (sort of abstract) is added. The angles of the various lines are determined by the vanishing points, with the exception of vertical lines which remain as vertical lines in the drawing.

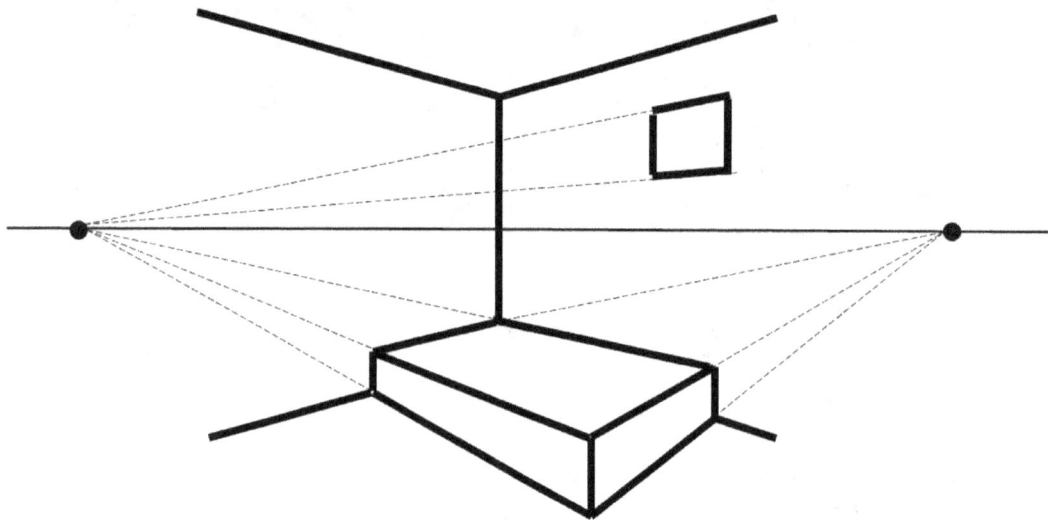

Figure 47. Drawing a room in two-point perspective – Step 2

In the third step (Figure 48), a door with a window and doorknob is added.

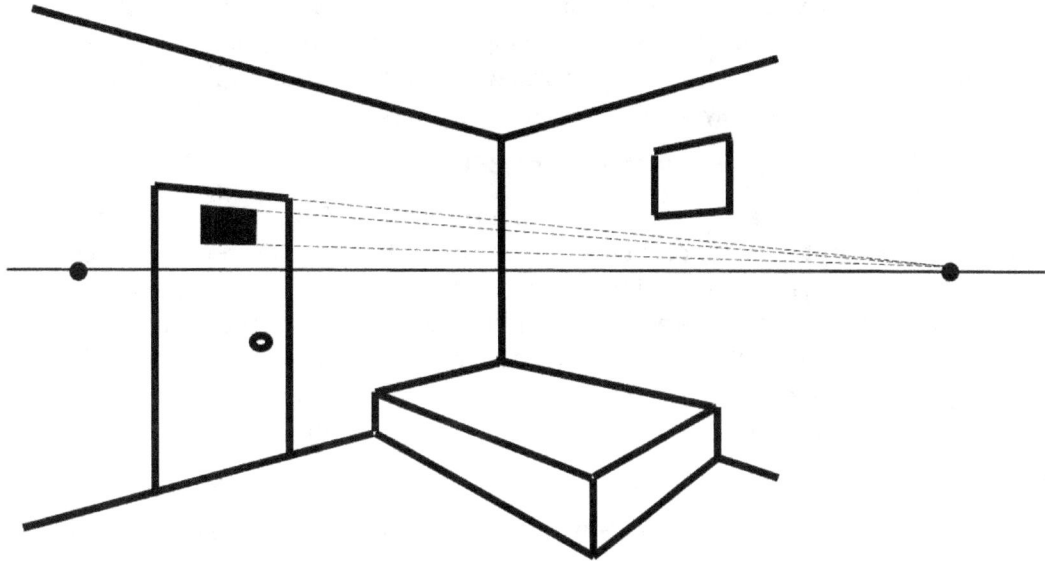

Figure 48. Drawing a room in two-point perspective – Step 3

For a more detailed and complex example of two-point perspective, see the YouTube video entitled "How to Draw a Building in 2-Point Perspective: Step by Steps" [32].

Less commonly used is something called 3-point perspective. The Merriam-Webster dictionary provides the following definition of 3-point perspective:

> Three-point perspective: linear perspective in which parallel lines along the width of an object meet at two separate points on the horizon and vertical lines on the object meet at a point on the perpendicular bisector of the horizon line.

Perhaps a bit more accessible is the definition from the Wikipedia article on perspective [29]:

> Three-point perspective is often used for buildings seen from above (or below). In addition to the two vanishing points from before, one for each wall, there is now one for how the vertical lines of the walls recede. For an object seen from above, this third vanishing point is below the ground. For an object seen from below, as when the viewer looks up at a tall building, the third vanishing point is high in space.

The YouTube video entitled "How to Draw using 3-Point Perspective: Simple Buildings" [33] gives an excellent demonstration of how to draw a building in 3-point perspective.

4.4   Impact on Mathematics

4.4.1   Definitions

The study of perspective in art eventually led to the development of a branch of mathematics known as **projective geometry**. Project geometry deals with the properties and invariants of geometric figures under projection.

From the Encyclopedia Britannica [34]:

> Projective geometry, a branch of mathematics that deals with the relationships between geometric figures and the images, or mappings, that result from projecting them onto another surface. Common examples of projections are the shadows cast by opaque objects and motion pictures displayed on a screen.

From the Wikipedia article on projective geometry [35]:

> Projective geometry is an elementary non-metrical form of geometry, meaning that it is not based on a concept of distance. In two dimensions it begins with the study of configurations of points and lines. That there is indeed some geometric interest in this sparse setting was first established by Desargues and others in their exploration of the principles of perspective art … Projective geometry can also be seen as a geometry of constructions with a straight-edge alone. Since projective geometry excludes compass constructions, there are no circles, no angles, no measurements, no parallels, and no concept of intermediacy.

From the textbook on projective geometry by Coxeter [36]:

> Plane projective geometry may be described as the study of geometrical properties that are unchanged by central projection, which is essentially what happens when an artist draws a picture of a tiled floor on a vertical canvas.

From the textbook by Ayers [37] (not so much a definition but more of a scope statement for his book):

> It has been noted that Euclid's geometry is not always the geometry of sight; for example, we never see parallel lines. If one stands midway [on] the rails of a straight railroad track, the rails appear to meet at a point on the horizon. Moreover, if a camera is used, the resulting picture will show the same phenomenon. Our concern from now on will be with the geometry, roughly of photography, called projective geometry.

4.4.2   Some Basic Concepts and Results

As suggested in the quote from Ayers in the previous section, projective geometry treats lines differently than in the Euclidean geometry that most of us learned in high school. In fact, parallel lines do not exist in projective geometry. In projective geometry, each line is extended by what is called an **ideal point** (or point at infinity). What would be two parallel lines in Euclidean geometry intersect at a common ideal point in projective geometry. The collection of all ideal points in the projective plane comprises what is called the **ideal line** for the plane. Similarly, there are no parallel planes in projective geometry. What would be two parallel planes in Euclidean geometry intersect at a common ideal line in projective geometry. These extensions lead to the following axioms concerning points, lines and planes in projective geometry:

1. Any two distinct points determine a unique line.

2. Any three distinct, non-collinear points (or one line and a point not on the line) determine a unique plane.

3. Any two distinct coplanar lines determine a unique point (could be an ideal point).

4. Any line not contained in a given plane intersects the plane in exactly one point (could be an ideal point).

5. Any two distinct planes intersect in exactly one line (could be an ideal line).

Notice that Axiom #3 is just Axiom #1 with "point" and "line" exchanged. This is not an accident. Something called the **principle of duality** holds for all axioms, definitions and theorems in projective geometry. The following quote from the Wikipedia article on project geometry [35] provides both a definition and some history on the concept of duality in project geometry:

> In 1825, Joseph Gergonne noted the principle of duality characterizing projective plane geometry: given any theorem or definition of that geometry, substituting "point" for "line", "lie on" for "pass through", "collinear" for "concurrent", "intersection" for "join", or vice versa, results in another theorem or valid definition, the "dual" of the first. Similarly, in 3 dimensions, the duality relation holds between points and planes, allowing any theorem to be transformed by swapping "point" and "plane", [and] "is contained by" and "contains". More generally, for projective spaces of dimension N, there is a duality between the subspaces of dimension R and dimension N−R−1. For N = 2, this specializes to the most commonly known form of duality— that between points and lines. The duality principle was also discovered independently by Jean-Victor Poncelet.

. . .

In order to tie this discussion to perspective in art, a few more definitions are needed:

- The set of points on a line is called a **pencil of points**. Similarly, the set of lines on (i.e., intersecting) a point is called a **pencil of lines**.

- Two pencils (of points or lines) are said to be in a **one-to-one correspondence** if there exists a rule which associates each element of one pencil with a unique element in the other pencil, and vice versa.

Figure 49 depicts a one-to-one correspondence between the pencil of lines on point X and the pencil of points on the line y. To be clear, only some of the points and lines are shown as there are an infinite number of lines and points in each pencil. The type of one-to-one correspondence shown in the figure is known as a **perspectivity** and is represented as $X(a,b,c,d,...) \overset{=}{\wedge} y(A,B,C,D,...)$.

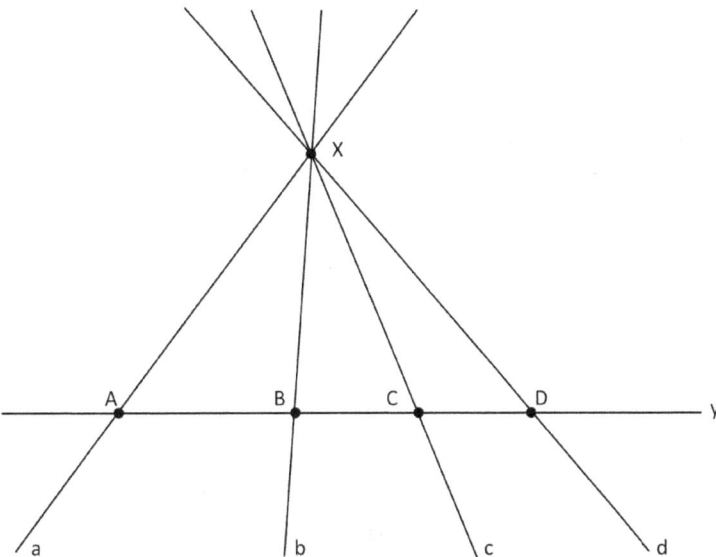

Figure 49. One-to-one correspondence between two pencils

Perspectivities can be chained to together to form what is called a **projectivity**. Figure 50 shows two projectivities, i.e., $X(a,b,c,d,...) \stackrel{=}{\wedge} y(A,B,C,D,...)$ and $X(a,b,c,d,...) \stackrel{=}{\wedge} z(A',B',C',D',...)$. Thus, we have $y(A,B,C,D,...) \stackrel{=}{\wedge} X(a,b,c,d,...) \stackrel{=}{\wedge} z(A',B',C',D',...)$ which gives us the projectivity $y(A,B,C,D,...) \stackrel{-}{\wedge} z(A',B',C',D',...)$. Note the $\stackrel{=}{\wedge}$ is used for perspectivities and $\stackrel{-}{\wedge}$ is used for projectivities. A projectivity is a string of concatenated perspectivities.

If (in Figure 50) the line segment from D' to A' is imagined to be an horizontal slice across the sensor of a camera, X to be the pinhole aperture of the camera, and line y to be a horizontal slice of a scene in the distance, then the projectivity can be seen as a representation of how light rays (represented by lines) map points in the scene to points on the camera's sensor.

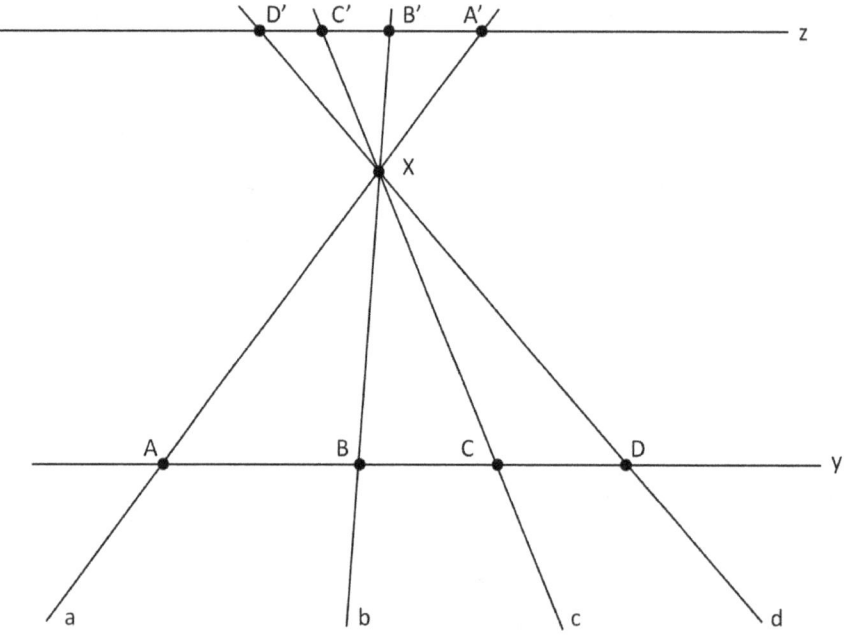

Figure 50. Example projectivity

We conclude this section with a few key results from projective geometry. For more complete coverage of the topic see the books by Ayers [37] or Coxeter [36].

As the name suggests, the next theorem is fundamental to projective geometry and is used in the proof of many other theorems.

Theorem 4-1 (Fundamental Theorem of Projective Geometry) Given three distinct collinear points (A, B, C) in a plane and another three distinct collinear points (A', B', C') on the same or a distinct line from (A, B, C), there is one and only one projectivity which maps the (A, B, C) to (A', B', C'), respectively.

A proof of this theorem can be found in Chapter 4 of Coxeter's book "Projective Geometry" [36].

One needs to be careful with the interpretation of Theorem 4-1. It is <u>not</u> saying that one cannot create multiple sequences of perspectivities (each sequence comprising a projectivity) that result in the mapping of (A, B, C) to (A', B', C'), respectively. It is saying that if X is any other point on the same line as A, B and C, then irrespective of the sequence of perspectivities comprising the projectivity from (A, B, C) to (A', B', C'), X is always mapped to the same point X'.

Given the principle of duality, we also have the following statement (equivalent to Theorem 4 1). Note that concurrent lines are defined as lines that intersect at one point.

> Given three distinct concurrent lines (a, b, c) in a plane and another three distinct concurrent lines (a', b', c') on the same or a distinct point, there is one and only one projectivity which maps lines a, b, c to a', b', c', respectively.

Next, we turn our attention to a famous theorem from projective geometry attributed to the mathematician Girard Desargues (1591 – 1661). First, consider the triangles ABC and A'B'C' in Figure 51. The triangles are said to be perspective from the P point since there is a one-to-one correspondence between the two triangles and the triangles are situated such that pairs of corresponding vertices are on concurrent lines, i.e., lines AA', BB' and CC' intersect at point P.

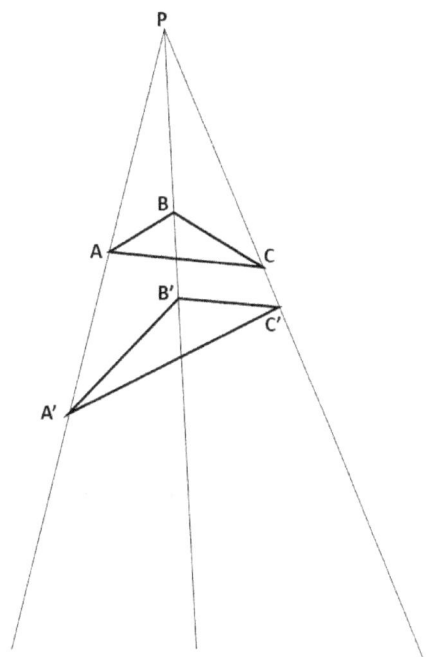

Figure 51. Triangles perspective from a point

As can be seen in Figure 52 (at least from appearance), the intersection points of the lines from corresponding sides of triangles ABC and A'B'C' (i.e., points D, E and F) all lie on a line. By Desargues two-triangle theorem (see Theorem 4-2), this is always true.

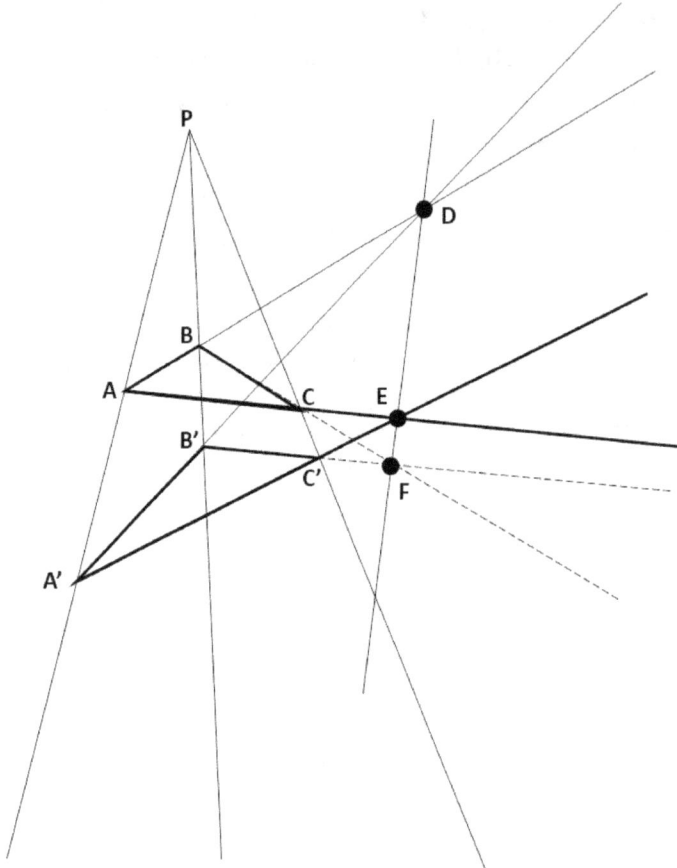

Figure 52. Example of Desargues two-triangle theorem

Theorem 4-2 (Desargues' Two-Triangle Theorem) If two coplanar triangles ABC and A'B'C' are perspective from a point P, then they are perspective from a line p, and conversely.

The "and conversely" phrase means that if the three points of intersection from lines extending from corresponding sides of two triangles all lie on the same line, then the two triangle are perspective from a point.

The YouTube video entitled "Desargues' Triangle Theorem" [38] provides an excellent visual presentation of the Desargues two-triangle theorem. The converse of the theorem is also illustrated near the end of the video.

Desargues two-triangle theorem is typical of the unexpected results that can be proven in the context of projective geometry.

Another well-known result is Pappus' hexagon theorem, attributed to Pappus of Alexandria (circa 290 – 350 AD).

Theorem 4-3 (Pappus' Hexagon Theorem) Given a set of collinear points A,B and C, and another set of collinear points A', B' and C' then the intersection points X,Y,Z of line pairs are collinear, lying on what is called the Pappus line.

While it is hard to visualize, the points X, Y and Z are the points of intersection of the opposite sides of the hexagon AB'CA'BC' (thus the name of the theorem).

Figure 53 depicts one of an infinite number of configurations that satisfy the conditions of Pappus' hexagon theorem. For an animation of the theorem, see YouTube video "Pappus's Hexagon Theorem" [39].

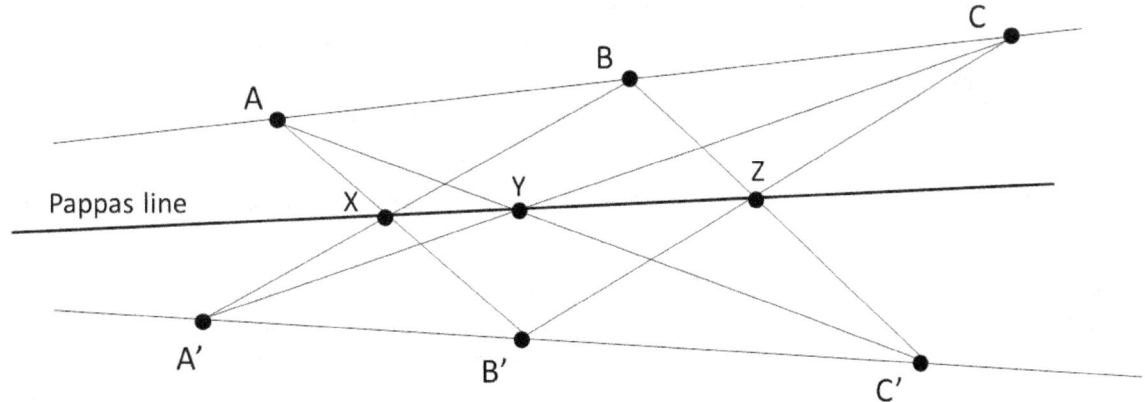

Figure 53. Example of Pappus' hexagon theorem

5   Optical Illusions

5.1   Overview

[**Author's Remark**: It is debatable whether optical illusions are mathematical, and some would question whether they should be considered as art.

At a very basic level, many of the optical illusions involve geometric shapes. Granted that this is a weak argument. In terms of science in general, the relationship is much stronger. There are many scientific papers concerning vision (or more precisely how our brain processes what we see) and the relationship to optical illusions. For example, see the paper by Edward Adelson entitled "Lightness Perception and Lightness Illusions" [40].

In my opinion, the case for optical illusion being considered as art is stronger than the case for optical illusions being seen as mathematical. For example, just do a search on "3D street art" and you will find a large collection of what are essentially optical illusions. The definition of art from the Free Dictionary by Farlex is quite broad and would also appear to include optical illusions:

> Art (noun) – The conscious use of the imagination in the production of objects intended to be contemplated or appreciated as beautiful, as in the arrangement of forms, sounds, or words.

Perhaps a more direct example is that of trompe l'oeil [41], an art technique that uses realistic imagery to create the optical illusion of a 2D image being 3D. An example of trompe l'oeil is shown in Figure 54. The so-called "melting building" is just a 2-dimensional painting on the façade of a building.]

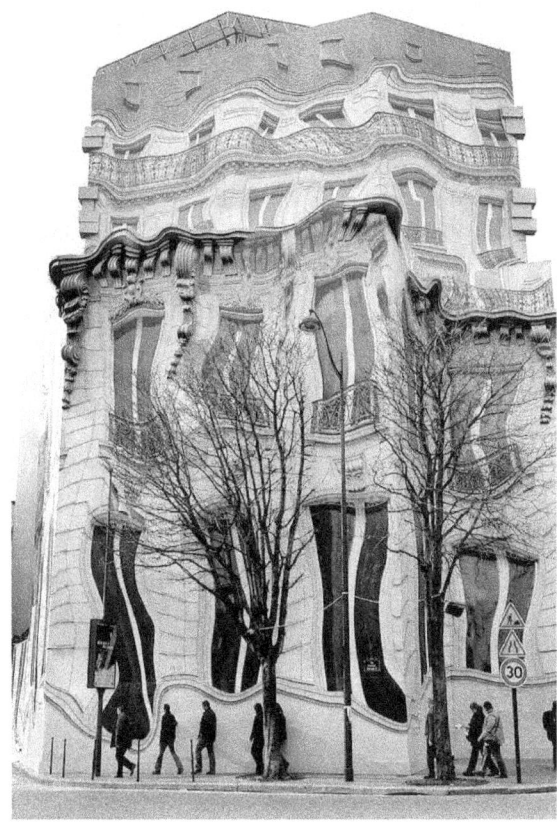

Figure 54. "Melting Building" at Georges V Ave. in Paris, France

This section covers optical illusions as perceived by human vision and the associated processing in the brain. An attempt is made to classify the various types of optical illusions. No deep insight is being claimed here with regard to the classification – just trying to be tidy and make things easier for the reader.

5.2   Impossible Shapes and Scenes

There are many examples of optical illusions concerning 2-dimensional drawings that depict objects that cannot possibly exist in our 3-dimensional world.

Figure 55 (known as an "impossible trident") shows a 2-dimensional figure, which is impossible in three dimensions. As noted in the book "The Art of Optical Illusions" [42], this figure started to appear in publications around 1964, but the original source is not known. See also the Wikipedia article entitled "Impossible trident" [43].

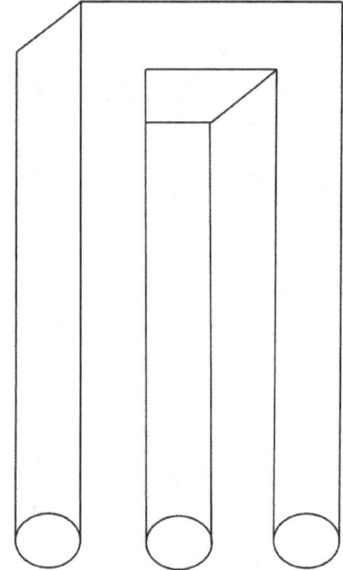

Figure 55. Impossible shape of unknown origin

Another impossible shape is the Penrose triangle, shown in Figure 56. The Wikipedia article entitled "Penrose triangle" [44] provides further background and a clever animation that reveals the nature of the illusion.

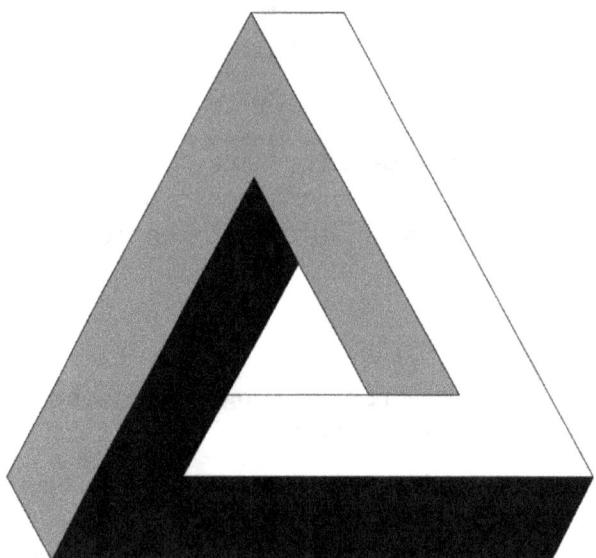

Figure 56. Penrose triangle

Similar in concept to the impossible triangle is the impossible circular shape shown in Figure 57.

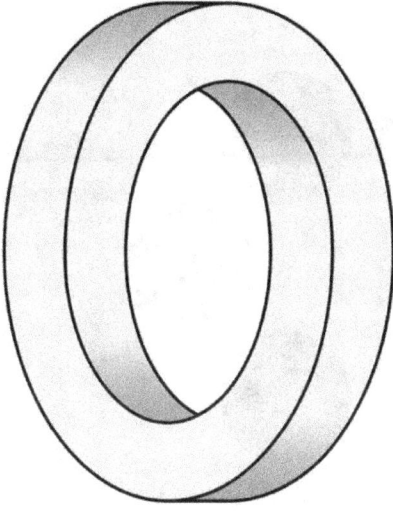

Figure 57. Impossible circular shape

M.C. Escher is famous for (among other things) his drawings of impossible scenes. See, for example, his lithograph "Waterfall" [45].

5.3   Color and Shading Illusions

The class of optical illusions in this subsection entail contrast and shading. Some of these illusions are hard for our brains to accept, but they are real. For example, the two vertical rectangles in Figure 58 are exactly the same color. This is known as White's illusion [46].

Figure 58. White's illusion

Perhaps less dramatic than White's illusion, but still hard to believe, is the Ebbinghaus illusion [47]. In Figure 59, circles A and B are the same size, but B looks larger since it is situated next to smaller circles.

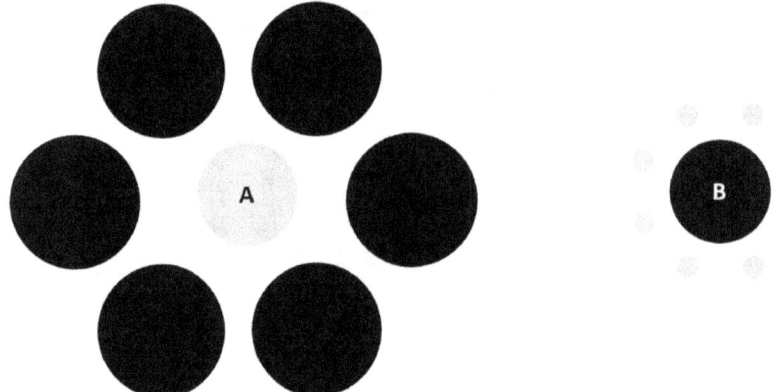

Figure 59. Ebbinghaus illusion

Our brains are apparently hard-wired to assume that light is coming from above, which is why the dots on the left of Figure 60 appear to be protruding out of the page and the dots on the right appear as depressions.

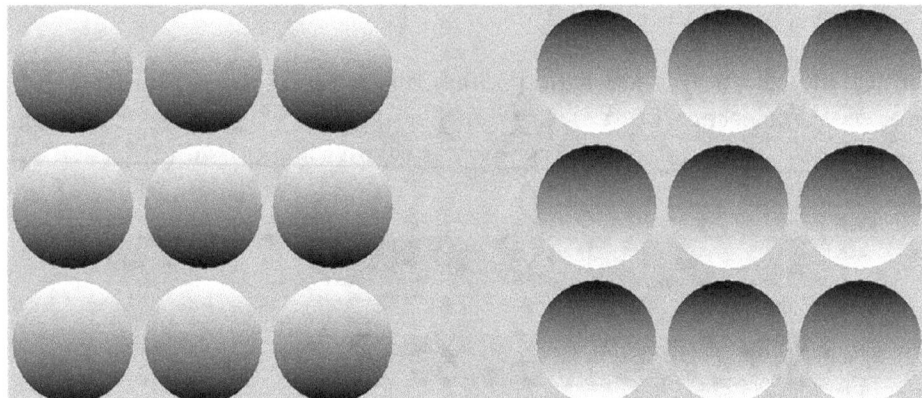

Figure 60. Assumed direction of light illusion

Many people find Adelson's checker-shadow illusion hard to believe. Tiles A and B in Figure 61 are exactly the same color. For a proof and an explanation of the illusion, see Adelson's webpage on the topic at http://persci.mit.edu/gallery/checkershadow.

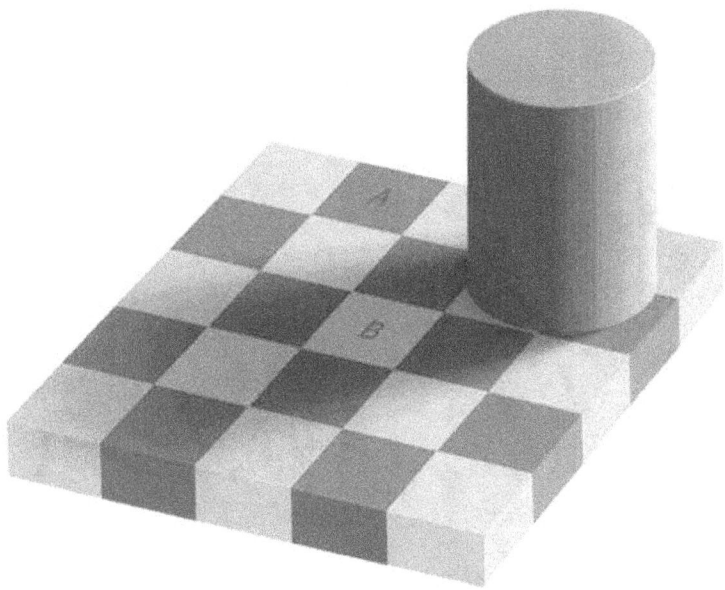

Figure 61. Adelson's checker-shadow illusion

The optical illusion in Figure 62 is similar in concept to Adelson's checker-shadow illusion. Again, tiles A and B are exactly the same color.

Credits for Figure 62 go to Henryk Żychowski, see https://commons.wikimedia.org/wiki/File:Optical_illusion.png.

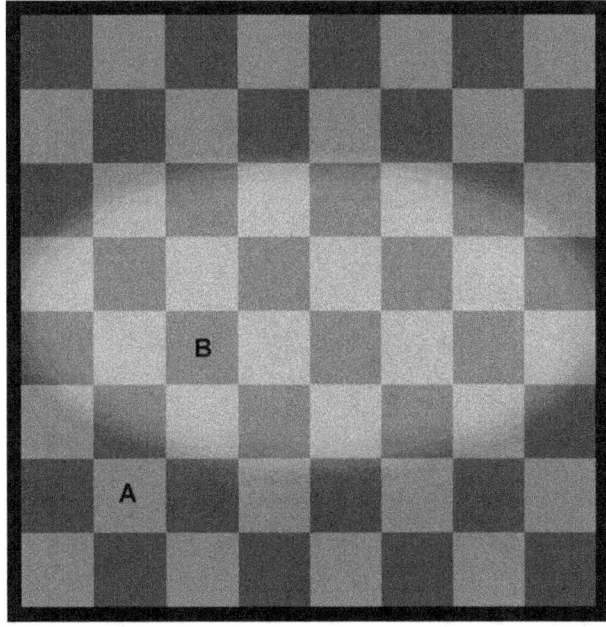

Figure 62. Optical illusion based on shading and position

Consider the two rectangles on the left-side of Figure 63. Rectangle B appears to be shaded darker on its right-side than on its left-side but Rectangle B is actually the same color and shading throughout. It is the shading of Rectangle A that causes this effect. The exact two rectangles are shown separately on the right-side of Figure 63.

Figure 63. Simple shading illusion

5.4   Size Illusions

Some of the simplest illusions involve the misperception of the relative size of objects. We have already seen an example of this type of optical illusion in Figure 59.

Figure 64 depicts a simple size distortion illusion. The two lines are the same length but the bottom line appears slightly longer.

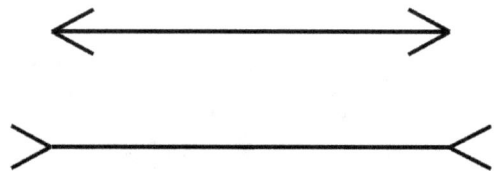

Figure 64. Simple size distortion illusion

Figure 65 is an example of a Ponzo illusion. The two vertical bars are of the same height but the one on the right appears longer. The Ponzo illusion [48] is a geometrical-optical illusion that was first demonstrated by the Italian psychologist Mario Ponzo (1882–1960) in 1911. He suggested that the human mind judges an object's size based on its background.

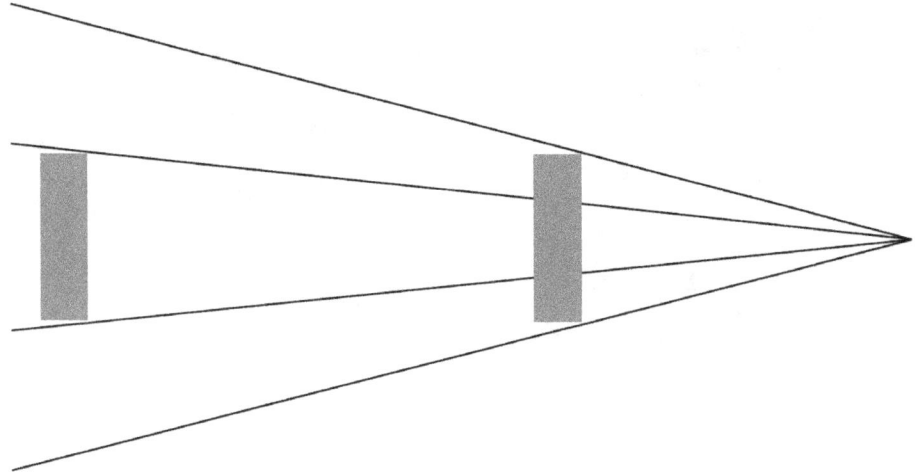

Figure 65. Example of a Ponzo illusion

One of the more difficult optical illusions to accept is known as Shepard tables [49]. The two tabletops in Figure 66 are exactly the same dimension. The front edge on each figure contributes to the illusion.

Figure 66 is from Wikimedia Common, see https://commons.wikimedia.org/wiki/File:Table_shepard.preview.jpg for the name of the contributing author and associated licensing information.

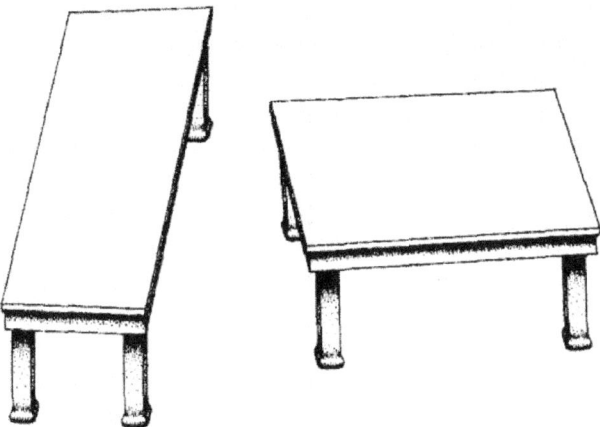

Figure 66. Shepard tables

5.5   Alignment and Shape Distortions

The next set of optical illusions concern misalignments (or more precisely, perceived misalignments).

In Figure 67, the diagram on the left gives the appearance that the solid line on either side of the rectangle is connected, but as can be seen in the diagram on the right, it is actually the dashed line on the right that continues through the rectangle to the solid line on the left. This perceived misalignment is known as the Poggendorff illusion.

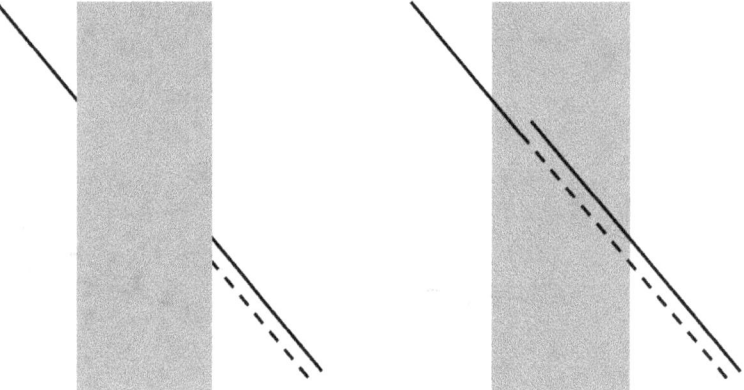

Figure 67. Poggendorff illusion

Figure 68 depicts a variation of the Poggendorff illusion. If the white rectangular bar is removed, a perfect circle is revealed.

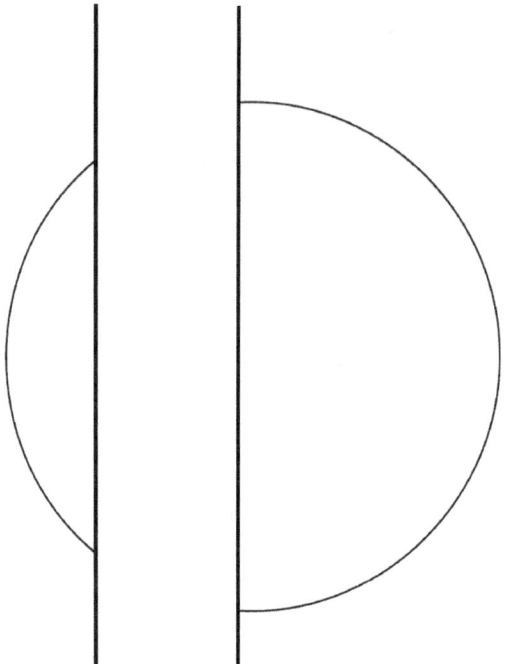

Figure 68. Circular Poggendorff illusion

The Wikipedia article entitled Poggendorff illusion [50] notes the following:

> The Poggendorff illusion is a geometrical-optical illusion that involves the misperception of the position of one segment of a transverse line that has been interrupted by the contour of an intervening structure. It is named after Johann Christian Poggendorff, the editor of the journal, who discovered it in the figures Johann Karl Friedrich Zöllner submitted when first

reporting on what is now known as the Zöllner illusion, in 1860. The magnitude of the illusion depends on the properties of the obscuring pattern and the nature of its borders.

Many detailed studies of the illusion, including "amputating" various components point to its principal cause: acute angles in the figure are seen by viewers as expanded though the illusion diminishes or disappears when the transverse line is horizontal or vertical. Other factors are involved.

Figure 69 depicts the Zöllner illusion (diagram credits to Fibonacci, see https://commons.wikimedia.org/wiki/File:Zollner_illusion.svg) . The diagonal lines are parallel but appear not to be.

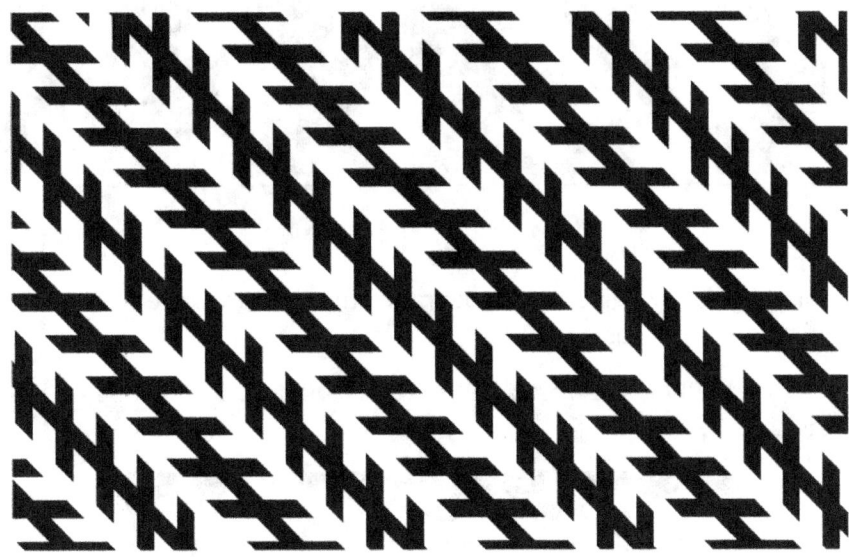

Figure 69. Zöllner illusion

The café wall Illusion (shown in Figure 70) gives the false impression that the horizontal lines are not parallel. However, the horizontal lines in the diagram are, in fact, parallel.

Credits for the figure go to W.A. Reiner, see https://commons.wikimedia.org/wiki/File:Café_Wall_Illusion.svg.

The Wikipedia article on this topic [51] provides the following historical background:

It was first described under the name Kindergarten illusion in 1898, and re-discovered in 1973 by Richard Gregory. According to Gregory, this effect was observed by a member of his laboratory, Steve Simpson, in the tiles of the wall of a café at the bottom of St Michael's Hill, Bristol. It is a variant of the shifted-chessboard illusion originated by Hugo Münsterberg.

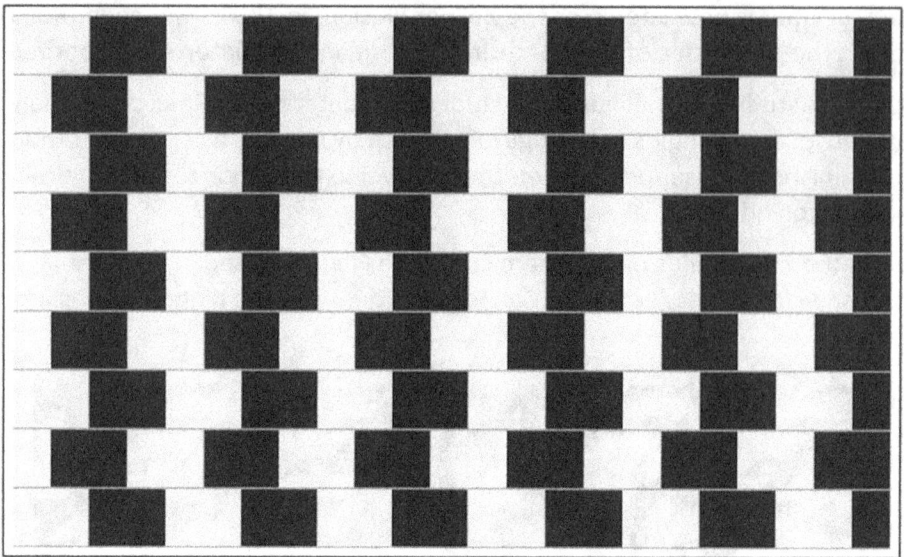

Figure 70. Café wall Illusion

The checkered board in Figure 71 gives the appearance that octagons are not lined-up at right angles but this is just an optical illusion.

Figure credits go to Tom Ruen, see https://commons.wikimedia.org/wiki/File:Optical-illusion-checkerboard-twisted-cord2.svg.

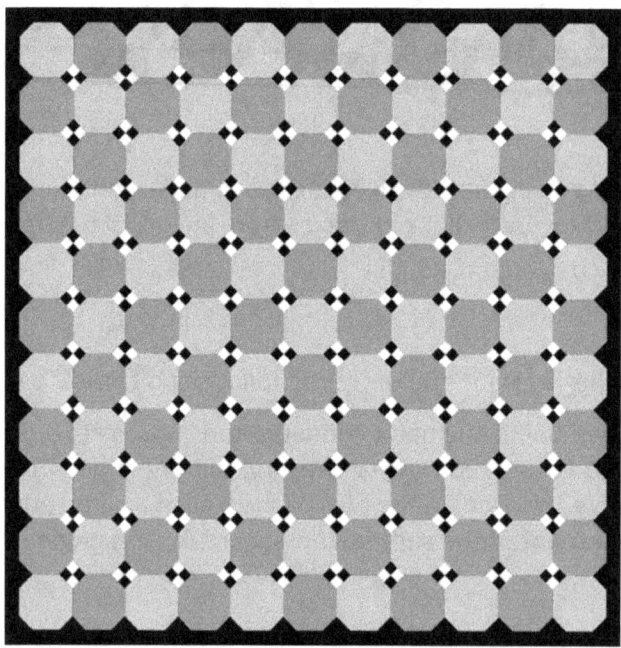

Figure 71. Twisted checkered board illusion

The Hering illusion, discovered by the German physiologist Ewald Hering in 1861, is simple and yet very effective (see Figure 72). The two vertical lines clearly look bent but are actually straight. The Wikipedia article on this topic [52] provides some possible reasons for the illusion:

> There are several possible explanations for why a perceptual distortion is produced by the radiating pattern. The illusion was ascribed by Hering to an overestimation of the angle made at the points of intersection. If true, then the straightness of the parallel lines yields to that of the radiating lines, implying that there is a hierarchical ordering among components of such illusion. Others have suggested that angle overestimation results from lateral inhibition in the visual cortex, while others have postulated a bias inherent in extrapolating 3D angle information from 2D projections.

> A different framework suggests that the Hering illusion (and several other geometric illusions) are caused by temporal delays with which the visual system must cope. In this framework, the visual system extrapolates current information to "perceive the present": instead of providing a conscious image of how the world was ~100 ms in the past (when signals first struck the retina), the visual system estimates how the world is likely to look in the next moment. In the case of the Hering illusion, the radial lines trick the visual system into thinking it is moving forward. Since we are not actually moving and the figure is static, we misperceive the straight lines as curved—as they would appear in the next moment.

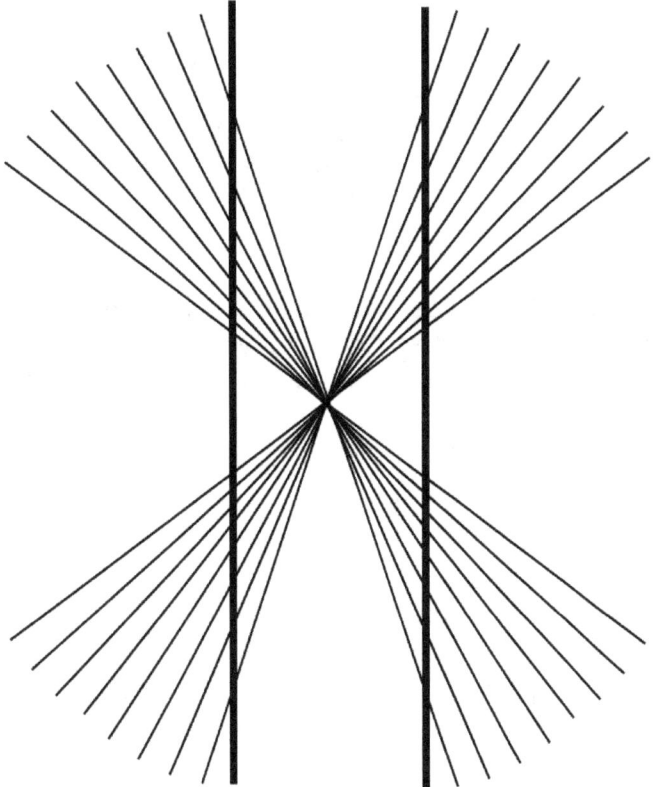

Figure 72. Hering's illusion

5.6   False Images

The optical illusions in this subsection trick the human mind into seeing objects or patterns that are really not there at all.

Figure 73 depicts an example of the Kanizsa triangle illusion. The Kanizsa triangle is named for the Italian psychologist Gaetano Kanizsa. Our brains impose a white triangle onto the drawing even though no such triangle has been drawn in the figure. Further, the nonexistent triangle appears brighter than the background.

The New World Encyclopedia article on this topic [53] provides the following explanation:

> The "phantom edge phenomena" (seeing an outline that is not actually there) is due to what neuropsychologists call the "T-effect." Groups of neural cells see breaks in lines or shapes, and if given no further input, will assume that there is a figure in front of the lines. Scientists believe that this happens because the brain has been trained to view the break in lines as an object that could pose a potential threat. With lack of additional information, the brain errs on the side of safety and perceives the space as an object. The circle is the most simple and symmetrical object, so the mind usually sees a circle unless active effort is made to see an alternate shape.

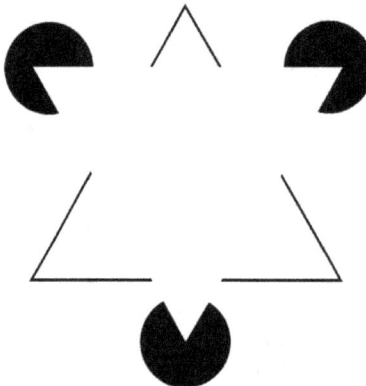

Figure 73. Kanizsa triangle

In the Ehrenstein illusion (Figure 74), we see small nonexistent circles at the intersections of the squares. The Ehrenstein illusion is named for German psychologist Walter Ehrenstein, who published his findings in 1941. This is another example of the phantom edge phenomena.

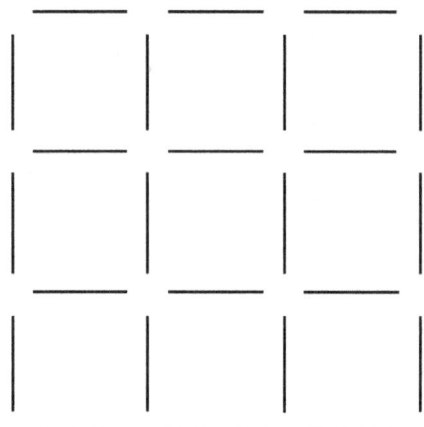

Figure 74. Ehrenstein illusion

The Fraser spiral (shown in Figure 75) is a series of concentric circles over a slanted checkered pattern that gives the appearance of a spiral. The Fraser spiral illusion was first described by the British psychologist Sir James Fraser in 1908.

From the Wikipedia article on this topic [54]:

> The visual distortion is produced by combining a regular line pattern (the circles) with misaligned parts (the differently colored strands). Zöllner's illusion and the café wall illusion are based on a similar principle, like many other visual effects, in which a sequence of tilted elements causes the eye to perceive phantom twists and deviations.

> The illusion is augmented by the spiral components in the checkered background. It is a unique illusion, where the observer can verify the concentric strands manually. When the strands are highlighted in a different color, it becomes obvious to the observer that no spiral is present.

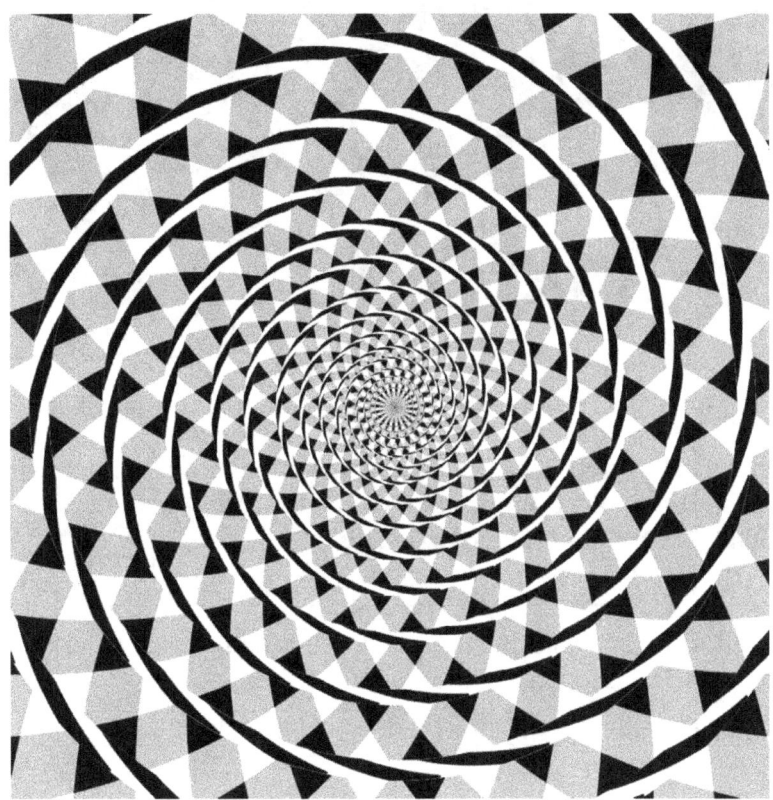

Figure 75. Fraser spiral

The illusion shown in Figure 76 was discovered by Baingio Pinna of the University of Sassari in Italy. The figure appears to contain intersecting spirals, but it is just a set of concentric circles. Further explanation of how the human visual system processes such a figure can be found in the article on Pinna's Intertwining Illusion [55].

Figure credits to Bernhard Wiedemann,
https://commons.wikimedia.org/wiki/File:Pinna%27s_illusory_intertwining_effect.svg.

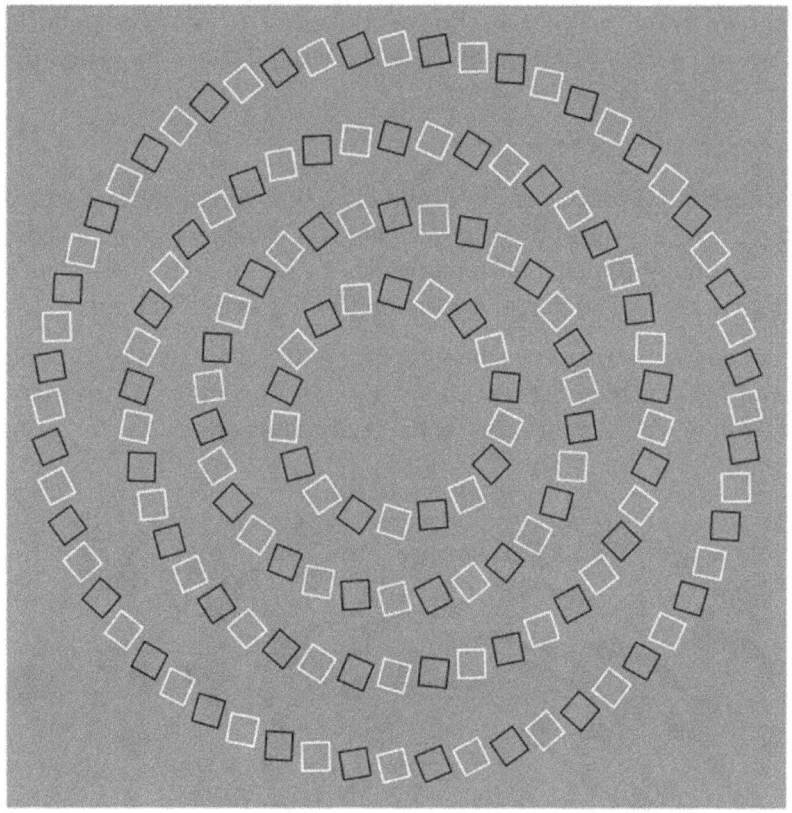

Figure 76. Pinna's intertwining illusion

5.7   False Depth Illusions

Another category of optical illusions includes art that gives the impression of depth or height. For example, there are many street art paintings that (when viewed from the correct angle) appear to extend into the ground. See the collection of paintings at

https://www.hongkiat.com/blog/absolutely-stunning-3d-street-art-paintings/

This approach also has practical applications. Some localities have used street art to calm or slow-down vehicle traffic. See the article on this topic at

https://www.fastcompany.com/90325319/this-optical-illusion-crosswalk-in-london-tricks-drivers-into-slowing-down

Figure 77 shows a simple example of the use of shading to give the impression of elevation. Notice that the spheres are in exactly the same position in the top and bottom portions of the figure, but the spheres on the bottom appear elevated off the ground because of the position of the shadows.

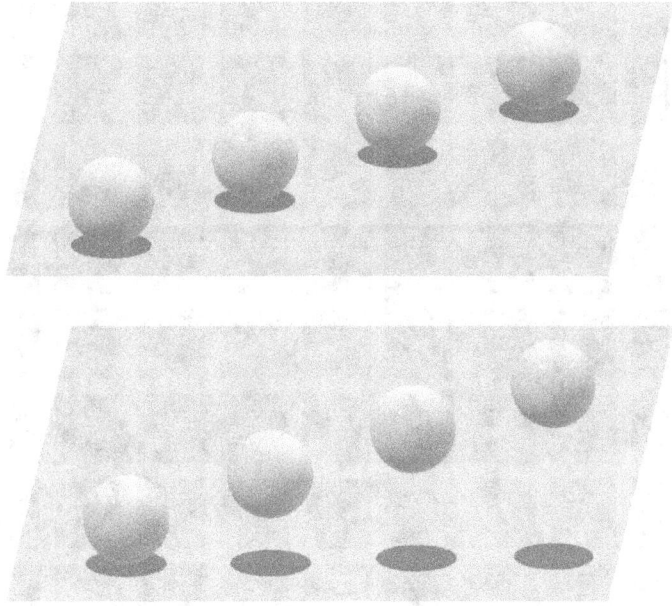

Figure 77. Use of shading to show elevation

5.8   Illusion of Movement

In this section, we discuss static drawings that give the appearance of movement when viewed by a human observer. [**Author's Remark**: I'm not sure if other animals see the same illusions. Probably nobody knows.]

Figure 78 shows an example of what is called a scintillating grid. If you move your eye about the drawing, dark dots appear and disappear rapidly at random intersections. However, if you stare directly at a single intersection, the dark dots do not appear. The scintillating grid illusion was discovered by Elke Lingelbach and M. Schrauf in 1994.

The effect of this optical illusion is sometimes explained by a neural process called "lateral inhibition." For other possible explanations concerning the cause of this effect, see the Theories section in the Wikipedia article entitled "Grid illusion" [56].

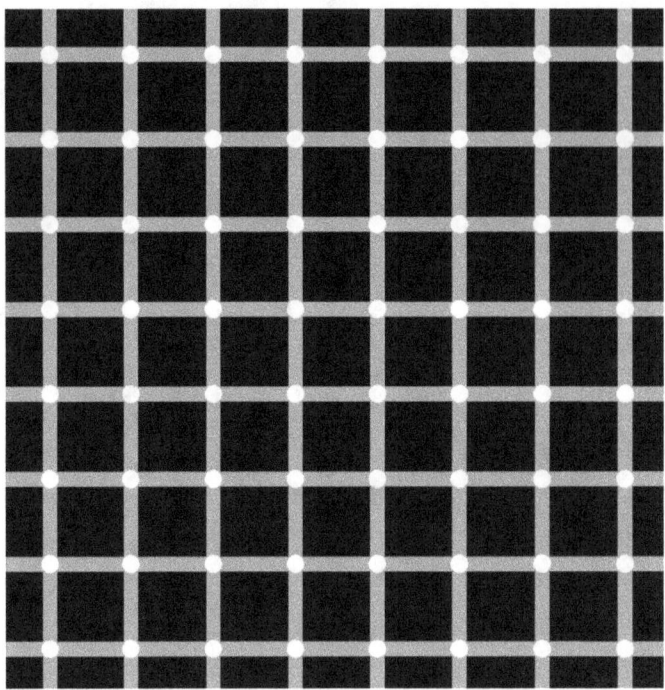

Figure 78. Example of the scintillating grid illusion

Pinna's rotating illusion is depicted in Figure 79. As you move your head towards and away from the figure the circles appear to rotate. Amazing, isn't it?

From the Scholarpedia article on Pinna's illusion [57]:

> The apparent rotation is typically perceived in peripheral vision. The looming in and out *[of your head with respect to the figure]*, with the gaze fixed not on the center but on any square, destroys the counter-rotation effect and the fixed square appears motionless. This is because motion detectors in the fovea are not sensitive to this type of stimulus pattern. Furthermore, with peripheral viewing the precise spatial square form of the pattern elements ought to be blurred and the dominant motion cues ought to derive, not from the constituent line sections, but from the entire elements

Figure credits to Fibonacci, see https://commons.wikimedia.org/wiki/File:Revolving_circles.svg.

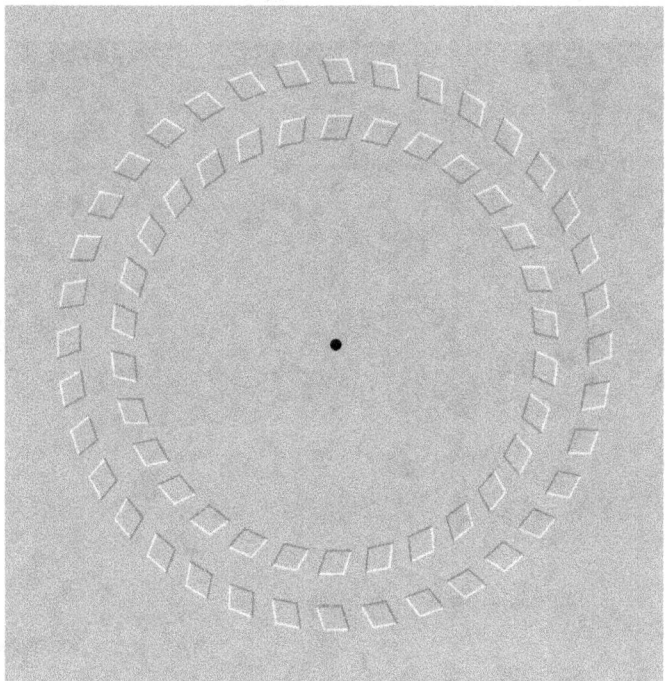

Figure 79. Penna's rotating illusion

Figure 80 depicts a rendition of the rotating snakes peripheral drift illusion. If you move your eyes about the figure, the various circles appear to rotate. As described in the Wikipedia article on the peripheral drift illusion [58]:

> Rotating Snakes is an optical illusion developed by Professor Akiyoshi Kitaoka in 2003. A type of peripheral drift illusion, the "snakes" consist of several bands of color which resemble coiled serpents. Although the image is static, the snakes appear to be moving in circles. The speed of perceived motion depends on the frequency of microsaccadic eye movements (Alexander & Martinez-Conde, 2019).

For additional moving optical illusions, see the website "Akiyoshi's illusion pages" at http://www.ritsumei.ac.jp/~akitaoka/index-e.html.

Credits for Figure 80 go to Cmglee, see
https://commons.wikimedia.org/wiki/File:Rotating_snakes_peripheral_drift_illusion.svg.

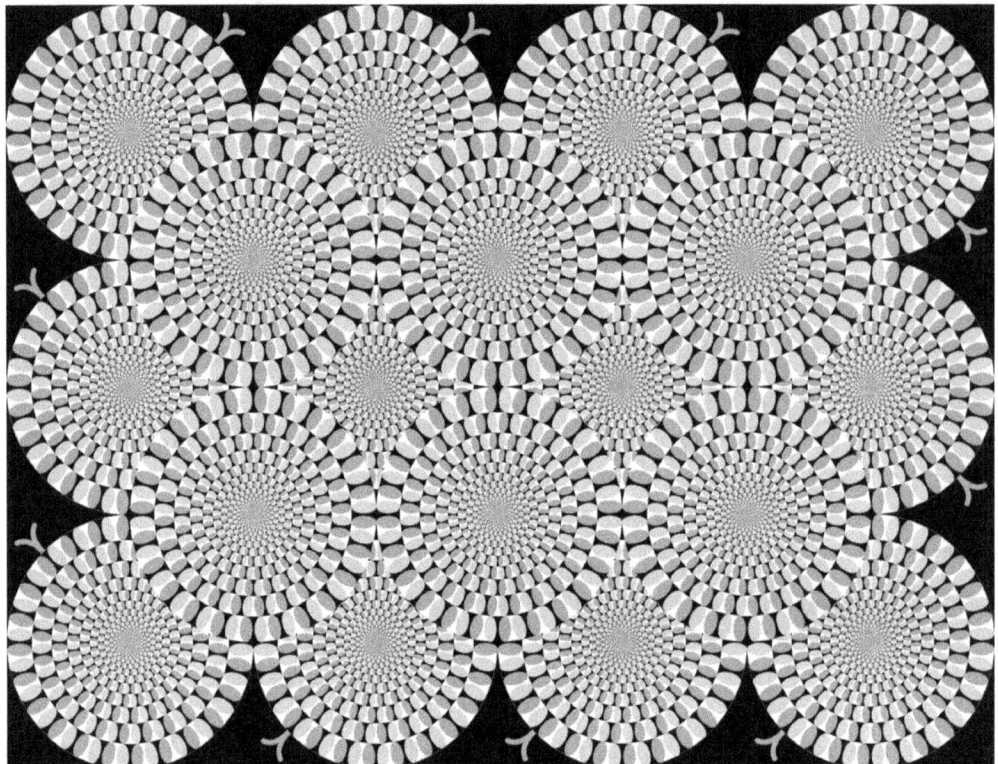

Figure 80. Example of a peripheral drift illusion

5.9   Famous Artists in the Realm of Optical Illusions

5.9.1   M.C. Escher

Maurits Cornelis Escher (1898-1972) was a Dutch artist who made mathematically inspired woodcuts, lithographs, and mezzotints. He is most famous for his so-called impossible structures, such as *Ascending and Descending*, *Relativity* and the woodcut *Metamorphosis I* (these works are copyrighted and so cannot be reproduced here, but are available for viewing at the official Escher online gallery at https://mcescher.com/gallery/). Although Escher was not trained as a mathematician, his work has a strong mathematical aspect. Several of his artworks made use of impossible objects such as the Necker cube and the Penrose triangle (see Figure 56).

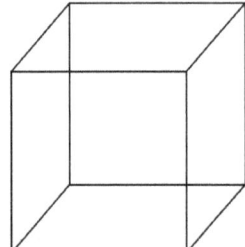

Figure 81. Necker cube

5.9.2 Bridget Riley

Bridget Louise Riley (born in 1931) is an English painter known for her singular "Op Art" paintings. (Op Art, short for optical art, is a style of visual art that uses optical illusions.) An example of her work is shown in Figure 82 (source: Wikimedia Commons, see https://en.wikipedia.org/wiki/File:Riley,_Movement_in_Squares.jpg). The repeated squares, gradually compressed from left and right, give a restless impression of movement, and refuse to let the eye settle.

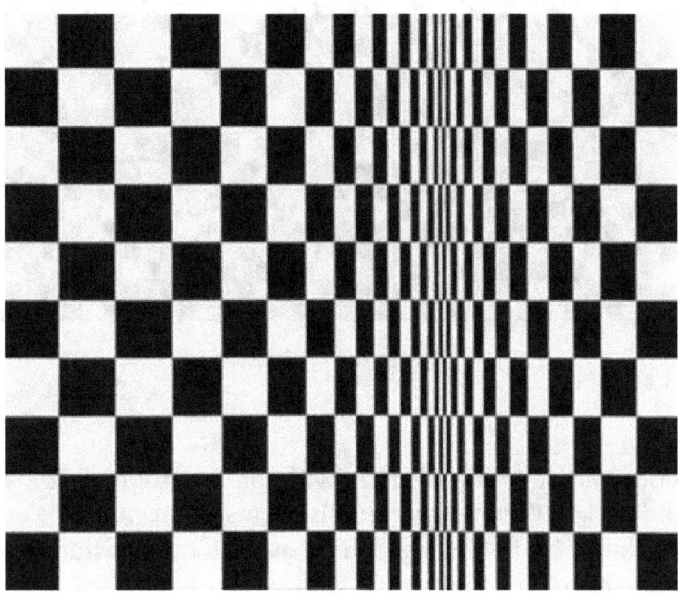

Figure 82. Movement in Squares (1961)

5.9.3 Victor Vasarely

Victor Vasarely (1906-1997) was an Hungarian-French artist who is generally recognized as the leader of the Op Art movement. His innovations in color and optical illusion have had a strong influence on many modern artists. An example of his artwork is shown in Figure 83. The article "Victor Vasarely: The art that tricks the eyes" [59] provides the following description of the drawing:

> The melting chessboard of Vasarely's elastic oil-on-canvas painting Vega (1956), created around the same time as Homage to Malevich, seems likewise committed not so much to measuring the weight and substance of what we actually perceive in the world around us, but, paradoxically, to offering a glimpse into the unseeable forces and gravities that twist and distort our perception. Here, it feels like the memory of the zebra's stretching and contracting stripes has been fed through a digitizing scanner or the pixelating mince of a particle collider in order to decrypt the binary code of its aesthetic essence.

The zebra reference in the above quote concerns a drawing by Vasarely known as Zebra (1937), see the WikiArt article on the topic [60].

(Credit for Figure 83: Belgique Photo/Photo: Philippe Migeat)

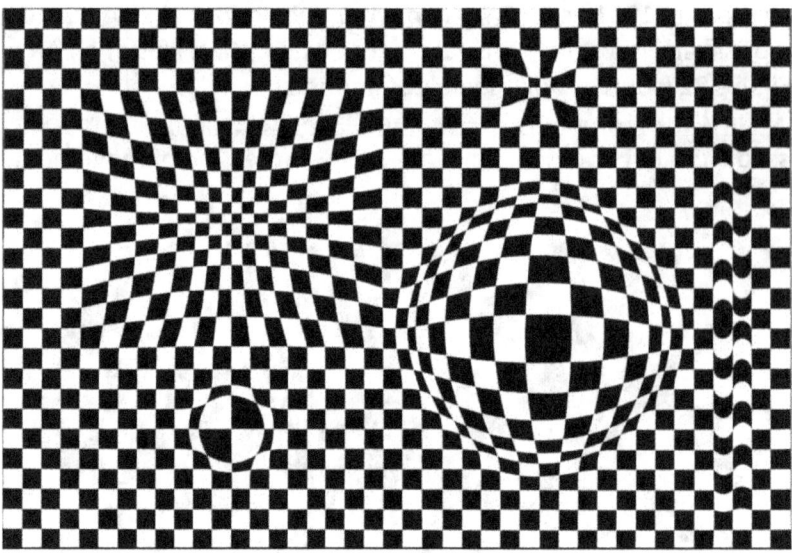

Figure 83. Vega, 1956

5.9.4   Kurt Wenner

Kurt Wenner is an American artist who is credited with the invention of 3D pavement art. After formal training in art and design, Wenner started his professional career as an illustrator for NASA. In 1982 he left NASA, sold all of his belongings, and moved to Italy to study the figurative drawing and art of the great artists from the Renaissance.

Figure 84 is an example of Wenner's 3D interactive art. The drawing is entitled Flying Carpet and it was drawn for the Corpus Domini celebration in Bettona, Italy. Notice the two children sitting on the drawing of a carpet, with the appearance of flying.

Figure credits: the photo comes from Wenner's web site and has been converted to grayscale for this book.

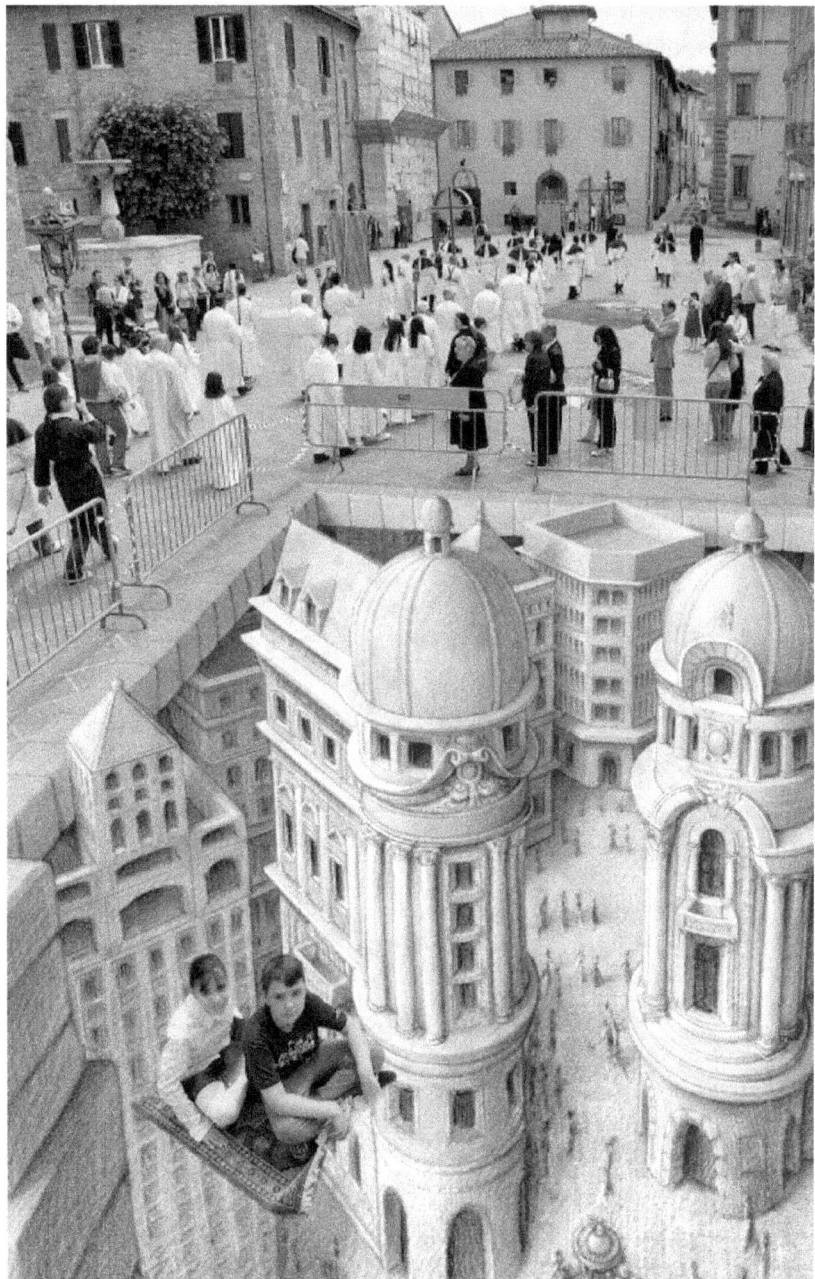

Figure 84. Flying Carpet (© 2011-2019 Kurt Wenner)

See Wenner's web site for a sampling of his many artworks (https://kurtwenner.com). Also, on Wenner's website, there is an excellent history of street art, 3D street art, and interactive 3D street art (see https://kurtwenner.com/history-of-3d-street-art/).

5.9.5   Edgar Mueller

Edgar Mueller is a German artist best known for his interactive 3D artworks. One of Mueller's works (The Crevasse) is shown in Figure 85. Mueller had the creation of this artwork recorded and then posted to YouTube (see https://youtu.be/3SNYtd0Ayt0). Notice the use of perspective in the construction shown in the video.

Figure credits are to Edgar Mueller, see
https://commons.wikimedia.org/wiki/File:The_Crevasse.jpg.

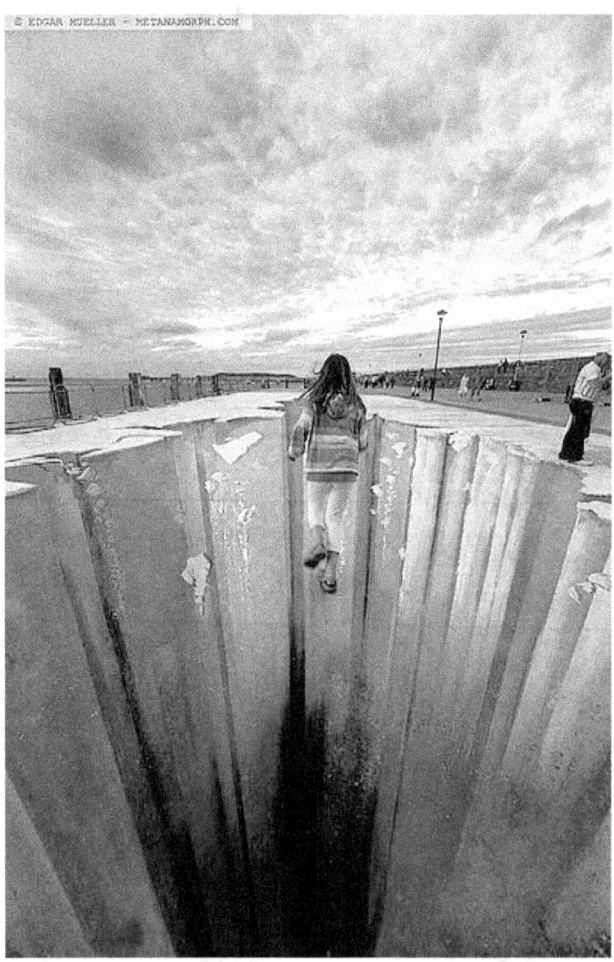

Figure 85. The Crevasse (2008)

5.9.6   Hamid Naderi Yeganeh

Hamid Naderi Yeganeh (1990) is an Iranian artist known for using mathematical formulas to create drawings of real-life objects, fractals and tessellations. As is the case with most of his drawings, Naderi Yeganeh's *Boat* drawing (Figure 86) is completely based on mathematical equations [61].

Naderi Yeganeh's approach is to generate thousands of drawings (via computer) and then select those that he finds most interesting. The article "Mathematics is Beautiful" [62] explains his general approach. The article "Mathematical Concepts Illustrated by Hamid Naderi Yeganeh" [63] provides some examples of his work along with the equations used to generate the images.

[**Author's Remark**: Hamid Naderi Yeganeh is not known for optical illusions. His work does not fit easily into any of the other sections of this book. I entertained various ideas for where to include a summary of his work and eventually decided on this section.]

Figure credit goes to Hamid Naderi Yeganeh, see
https://commons.wikimedia.org/wiki/File:Boat_by_Hamid_Naderi_Yeganeh.jpg.

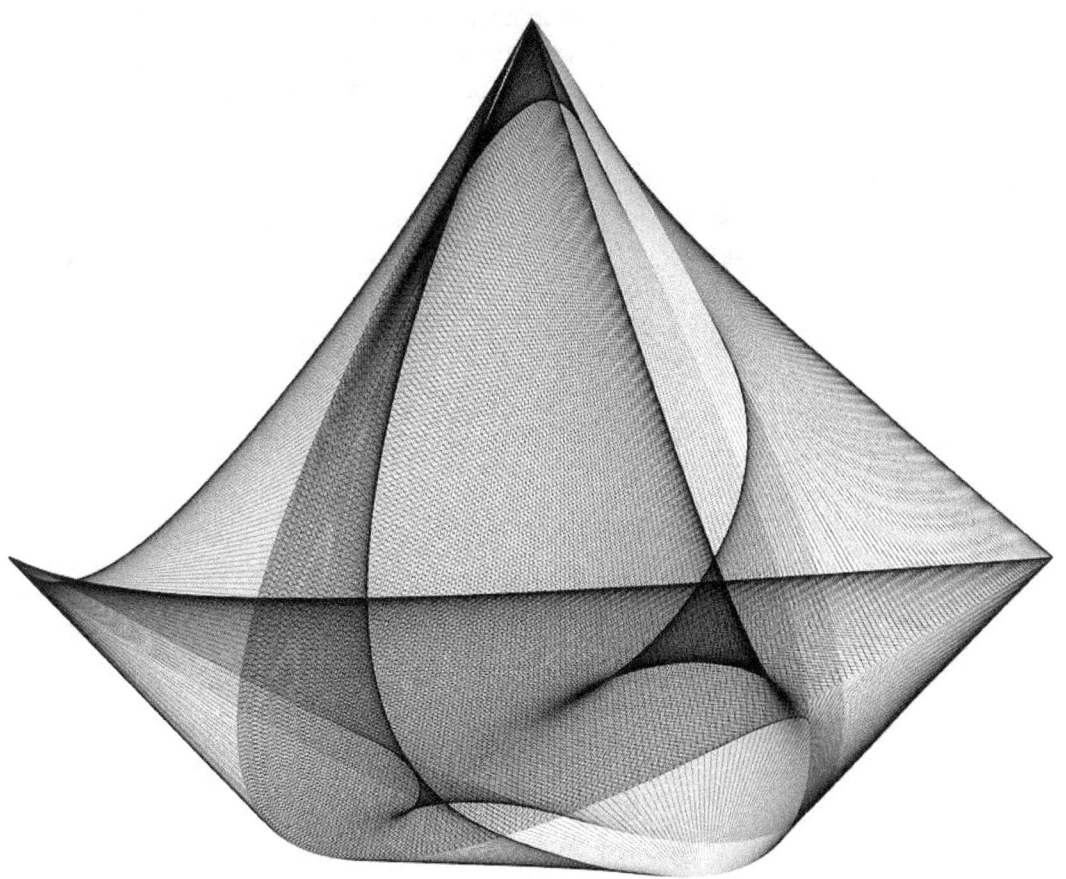

Figure 86. Boat (2015)

5.10 Moving Optical Illusions

Some of the most bewildering and fascinating optical illusions involve motion. Unfortunately, motion cannot be represented in a static book such as this. However, it would be remiss not to at least provide some references to optical illusions involving motion.

- The Ames Window Illusion entails a trapezoid-shaped window that appears to be oscillating back and forth, but is actually rotating. The YouTube video "The Illusion Only Some Can See" [64] provides an analysis of this illusion, along with some hard to believe (but real) video. This video also covers another illusion known as the Ames Room. Both illusions are attributed to American scientist Adelbert Ames, Jr. Also, see the Wikipedia article entitled "Ames trapezoid" [65].

- The YouTube video "Amazing Animated Optical Illusions! #7" [66] illustrates a technique that fools the eyes into seeing motion.

- **Anamorphosis** is a distorted projection requiring the viewer to occupy a specific vantage point, use special devices or both to view a recognizable image [67]. Basically, a 2-dimensional drawing is used to give the very real impression of a 3-dimensional object, but the drawing needs to be viewed from a precise vantage point. If the person viewing the image moves, the illusion is revealed. The YouTube video "Amazing Anamorphic Illusions!" [68] illustrates this concept very well.

- There is also something called mirror anamorphosis where an image is revealed only if viewed from a mirror. The article "23 Amazing Anamorphic Artworks That Need A Mirror Cylinder To Reveal Their Beauty" [69] provides a wonderful collection of this type of artwork.

- Animations (such as cartoons) are also a sort of optical illusion in the sense that a series of still images are perceived by the mind as continuous motion. The TED video entitled "Animation basics: The optical illusion of motion" [70] provides an explanation of this concept.

6   Patterns

6.1   Overview

This section is about various mathematical patterns that may be considered as art or, in some cases, as integral parts of artwork.

[**Author's Remark**: It is true that tessellations and fractals can also be considered as patterns, but I decided to put those topics in separate sections.]

6.2   Graphs

6.2.1   Coordinate Systems

First some background, then some interesting graphs in the next subsection …

The representation of points and sets of points on a graph entails the selection of a coordinate system. Figure 87 shows the representation of the same point in two different coordinate systems. On the left, is the more familiar Cartesian coordinate system. The point (1,1) is one unit along the positive x-axis and one unit in the positive y-axis. The same point (as shown in the right-side of Figure 87) can be represented by stating the distance from the origin (i.e., intersection of the two axes) and the angle from the horizontal axis as measured in the counterclockwise direction.

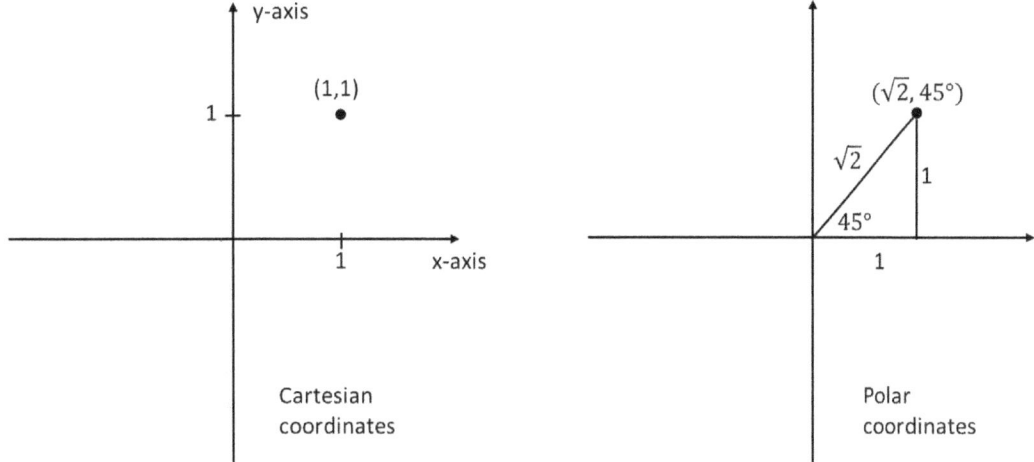

Figure 87. Representation of a point in two coordinate systems

The polar coordinate representation is more natural for the representation of some graphs. For example, it is easier and more natural to represent a circle in polar coordinates. The Cartesian coordinates representation for the circle in Figure 88 is

$$x^2 + y^2 = 1$$

but the polar coordinates representation is simply

$$r = 1$$

i.e., all the points that are distance 1 from the origin, regardless of the angle.

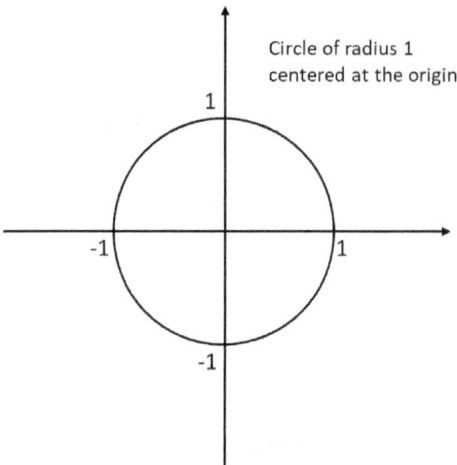

Figure 88. Graph of a circle

In three dimensions, the Cartesian coordinate system just adds another axis for height (called the z-axis) that is perpendicular to the plane of the other two axes. In polar coordinates, two angles and a radius are required to specify the location of a point (see Figure 89 and the associated Wikipedia article on coordinate systems [71]).

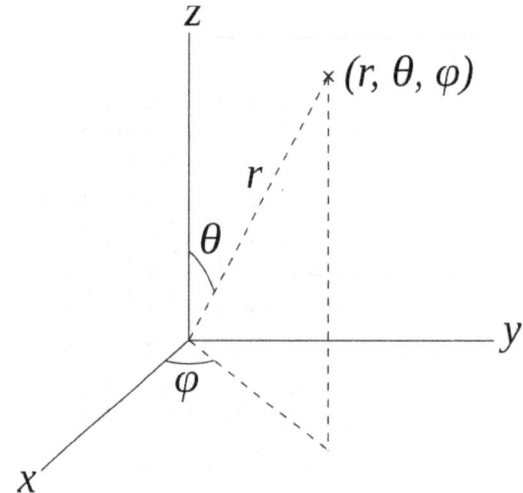

Figure 89. Polar coordinates in three dimensions

6.2.2   2-Dimensional Graphs

Among the artistic and easy to generate graphs are the spirals. With the exception of the Spiral of Theodorus, all the graphs in this subsection were generated using the online drawing application at https://www.desmos.com.

The Archimedean spiral (also known as the arithmetic spiral) is a spiral named after the 3rd-century B.C. Greek mathematician Archimedes. An example of an Archimedean spiral is depicted in Figure 90. In polar coordinates, the equation for this spiral is $r = \theta$. The spiral continues indefinitely but for the figure, $0 \le \theta \le 12\pi$ (which amounts to 6 revolutions). (Note that the angle θ is given in radians, where π radians is equal to 180 degrees.)

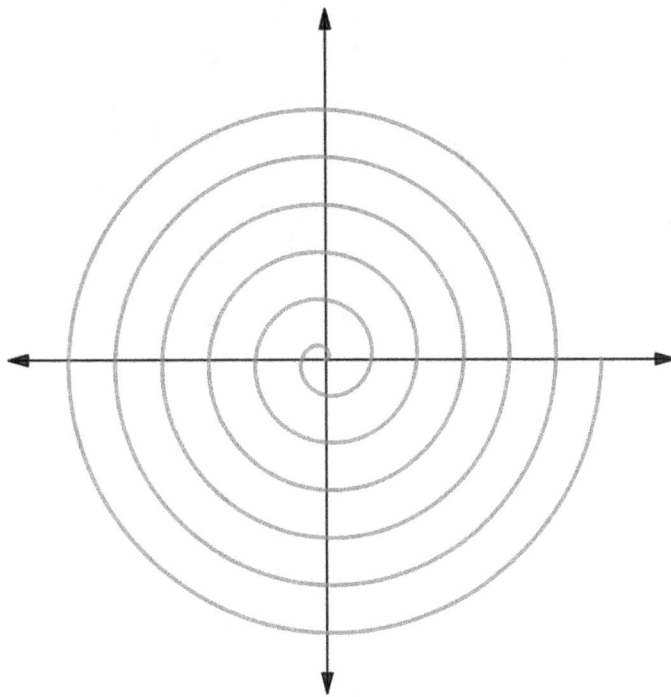

Figure 90. Archimedean spiral

An example of Fermat's spiral is shown in Figure 91. The spiral has two "arms" with one arm given by the equation (again in polar coordinates) $r = 3\sqrt{\theta}$ and the other by $r = -3\sqrt{\theta}$.

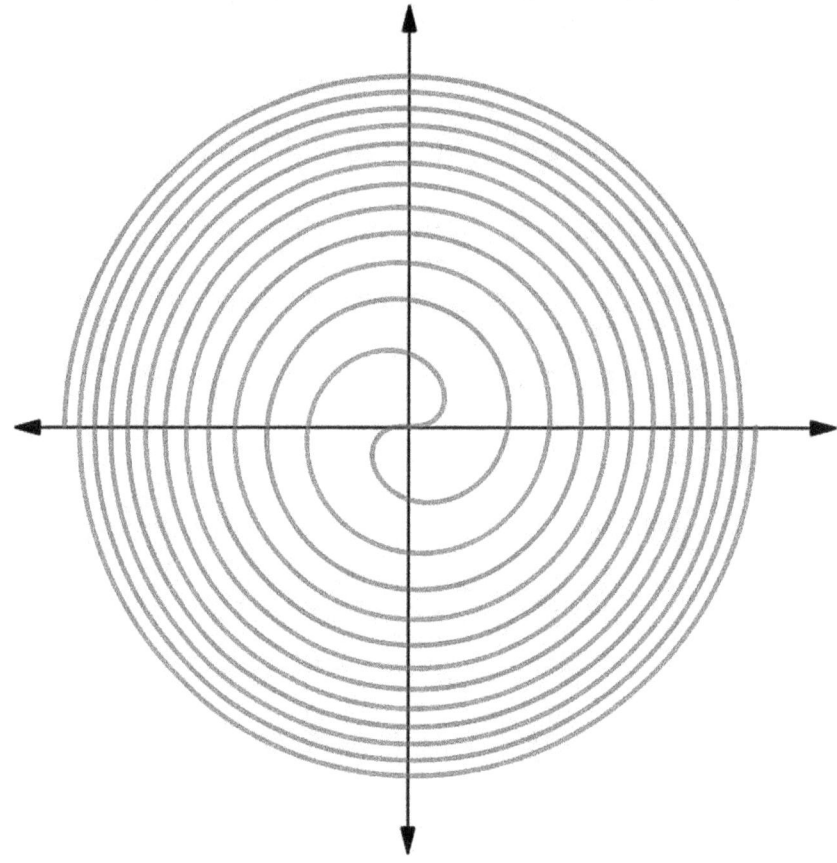

Figure 91. Fermat's spiral

Figure 92 depicts a hyperbolic spiral given by the equation $r = \dfrac{1}{\theta}$. The graph converges to the origin but for the figure, we have limited the angle, i.e., $0 \le \theta \le 12\pi$.

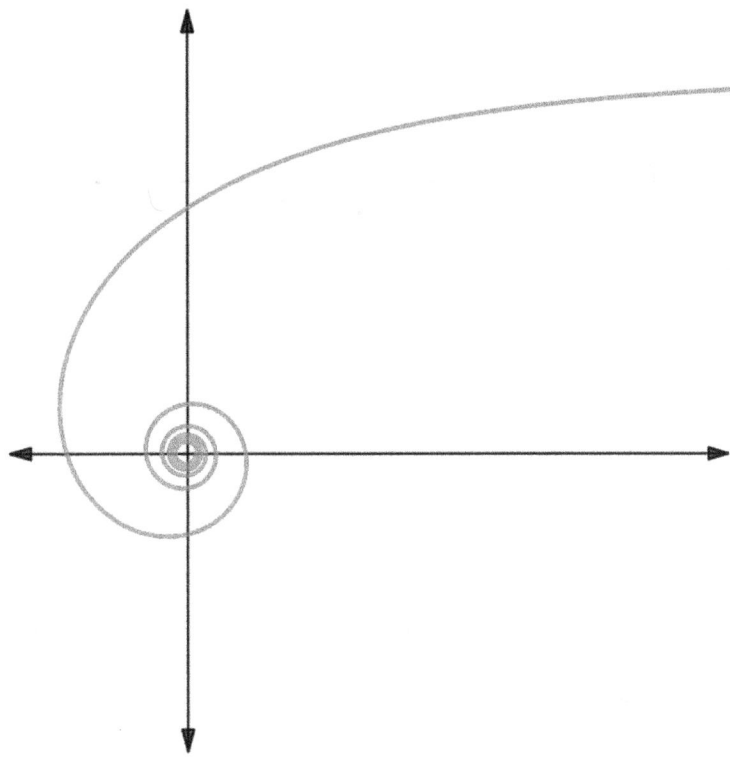

Figure 92. Hyperbolic spiral

A closeup of the hyperbolic spiral, with the restriction $0 \le \theta \le 12\pi$, is shown in Figure 93. If the upper bound on θ is lifted, the spiral continues to slowly converge to the origin.

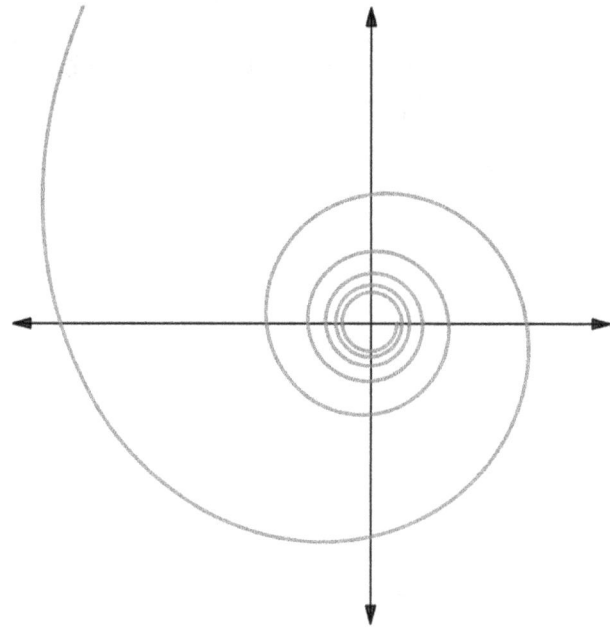

Figure 93. Closeup of hyperbolic spiral

The spiral of Theodorus (sometimes referred to as the square root spiral, Einstein spiral or Pythagorean spiral) is a graph composed of right triangles, placed edge-to-edge in a spiral fashion, as shown in Figure 94.

Figure credits go to pbroks13, see
https://commons.wikimedia.org/wiki/File:Spiral_of_Theodorus.svg.

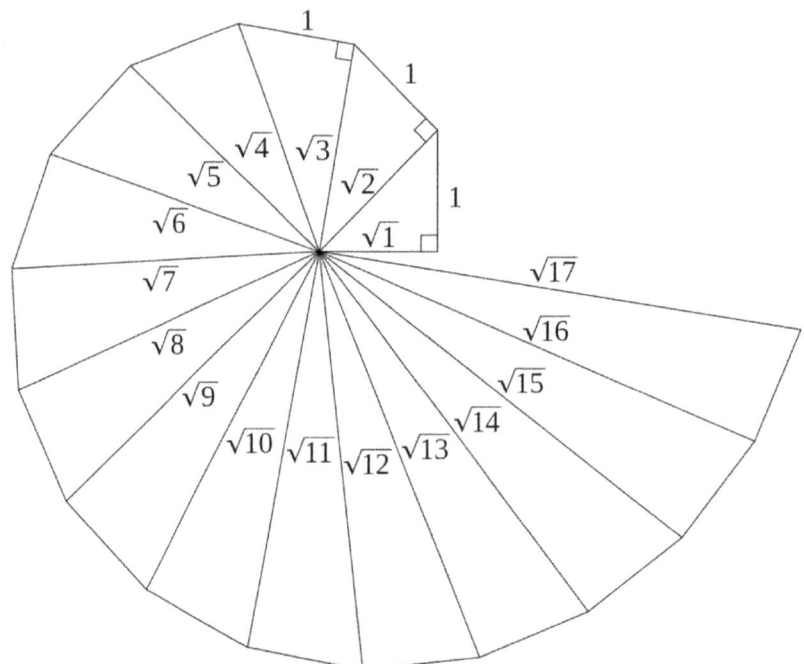

Figure 94. Spiral of Theodorus

The next two graphs entail the overlay of several cardioids. As stated in the Wikipedia article on cardioids [72]:

> A cardioid (from the Greek καρδία "heart") is a plane curve traced by a point on the perimeter of a circle that is rolling around a fixed circle of the same radius. It can also be defined as an epicycloid having a single cusp. It is also a type of sinusoidal spiral, and an inverse curve of the parabola with the focus as the center of inversion.
>
> The name was coined by de Castillon in 1741 but had been the subject of study decades beforehand. Named for its heart-like form, it is shaped more like the outline of the cross section of a round apple without the stalk.

See also the animation in the same Wikipedia article.

Two superimposed petal-shaped cardioids are shown in Figure 95. The dashed cardioid is the same as the solid line cardioid but rotated $\frac{\pi}{4}$ radians (i.e., 45 degrees). The equations for the dashed and solid line cardioids are as follows:

- $r = 3\sin(7\theta), 0 \leq \theta \leq \pi$
- $r = 3\sin(7\theta + \pi/2), 0 \leq \theta \leq \pi$

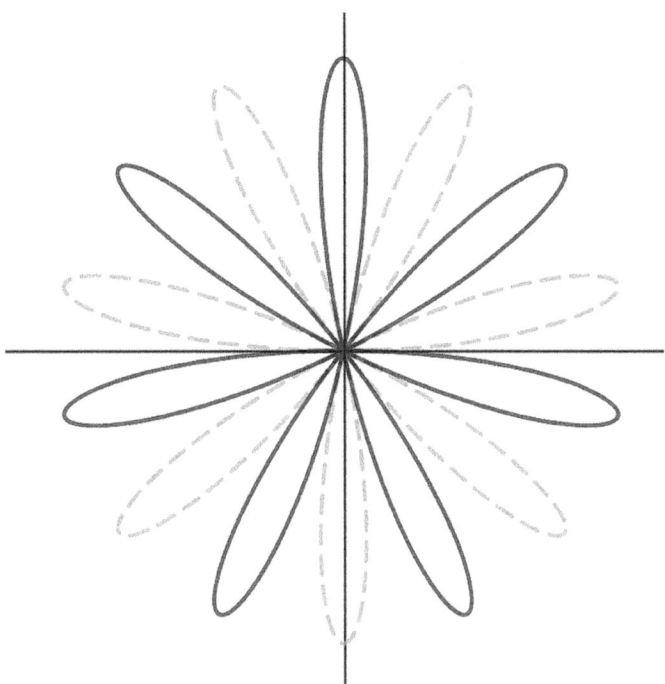

Figure 95. Two petal-shaped cardioids

Figure 96 depicts three superimposed cardioids. The equations are as follows:

- $r = \sin(7\theta), 0 \leq \theta \leq \pi$ (innermost petal)

- $r = \sin(7\theta) + 2, 0 \leq \theta \leq \pi$ (middle cardioid)

- $r = \sin(7\theta) + 4, 0 \leq \theta \leq \pi$ (outer cardioid).

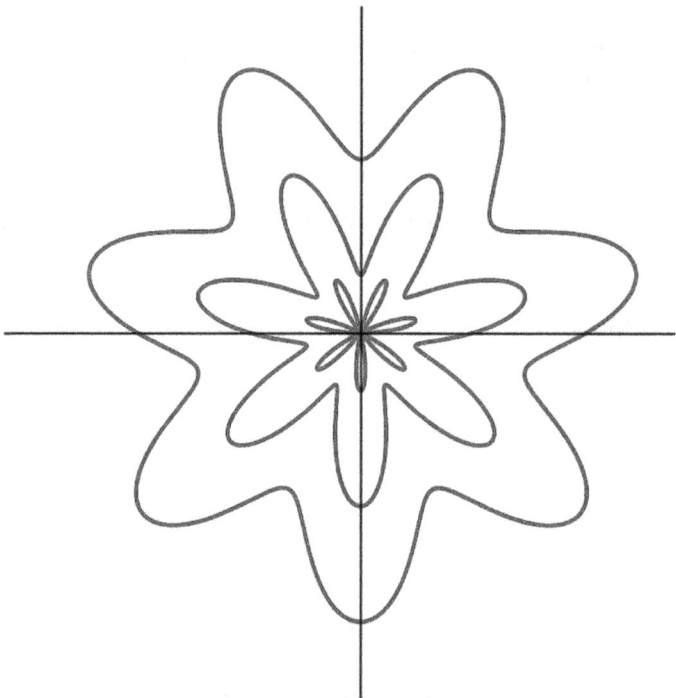

Figure 96. Three superimposed cardioids

Another way to express a graph is through parametrization. For example, we can represent $y = x^2$ with two equations using a common parameter t as follows:

$x = t$

$y = t^2$

For a more interesting example, consider the parametric equations:

$x = 16(\sin t)^3$

$y = 13\cos t - 5\cos 2t - 2\cos 3t - \cos 4t$

$0 \le t \le 2\pi$

This yields the heart-shaped graph in Figure 97. (The graph was created using the Desmos parametric graphing capability at https://www.desmos.com.)

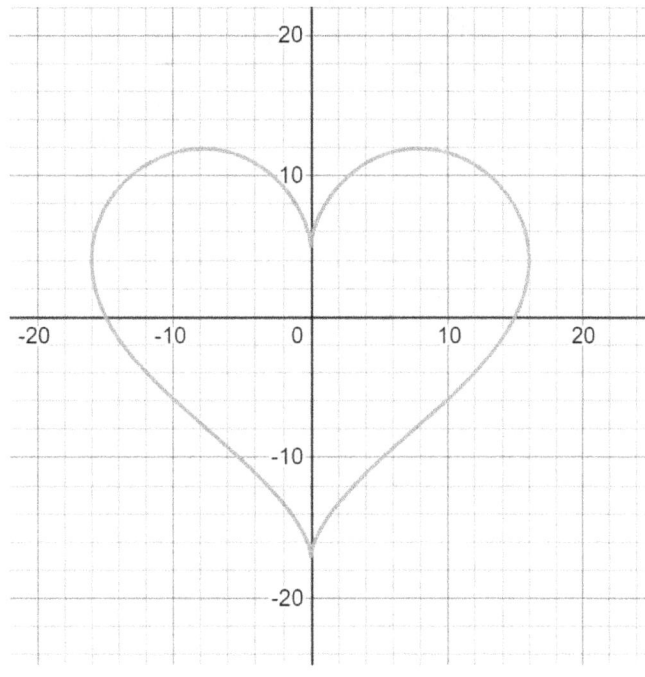

Figure 97. Heart-shaped graph

6.2.3   3-Dimensional Graphs

Graphs in 3-dimensions can also be artful but are much harder to draw by hand than 2-dimensional graphs. The graphs in this subsection were drawn using the Geogebra 3D Calculator at https://www.geogebra.org/3d. The static drawings in this subsection do not give full justice to the graphs. In order to fully appreciate and observe 3-dimensional graphs, one needs to be able to rotate the graph and view it from various angles (the Geogebra 3D Calculator allows one to do so).

Figure 98 depicts a sinusoidal surface using Cartesian coordinates. The equation for the graph is shown just below the graph.

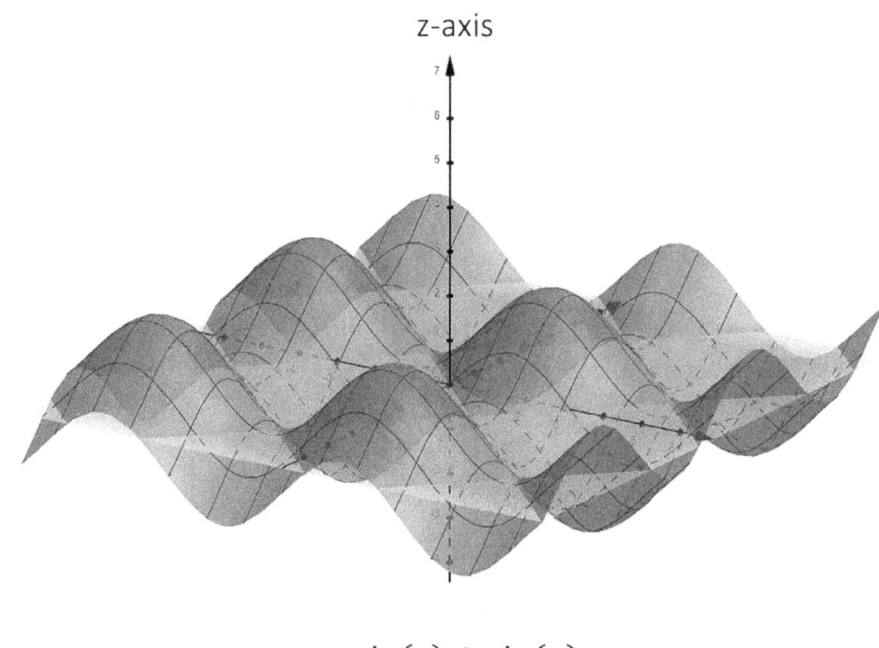

$$z = \sin(x) + \sin(y)$$

Figure 98. Three dimensional sinusoidal surface

Figure 99 depicts a graph based on the trigonometric sine function. The graph is reminiscent of ripples in a pond caused by throwing a stone into the pond. The Cartesian coordinate system is also used here. The equation for the graph is shown just above the graph.

$$z = \sin(x^2 + y^2)$$

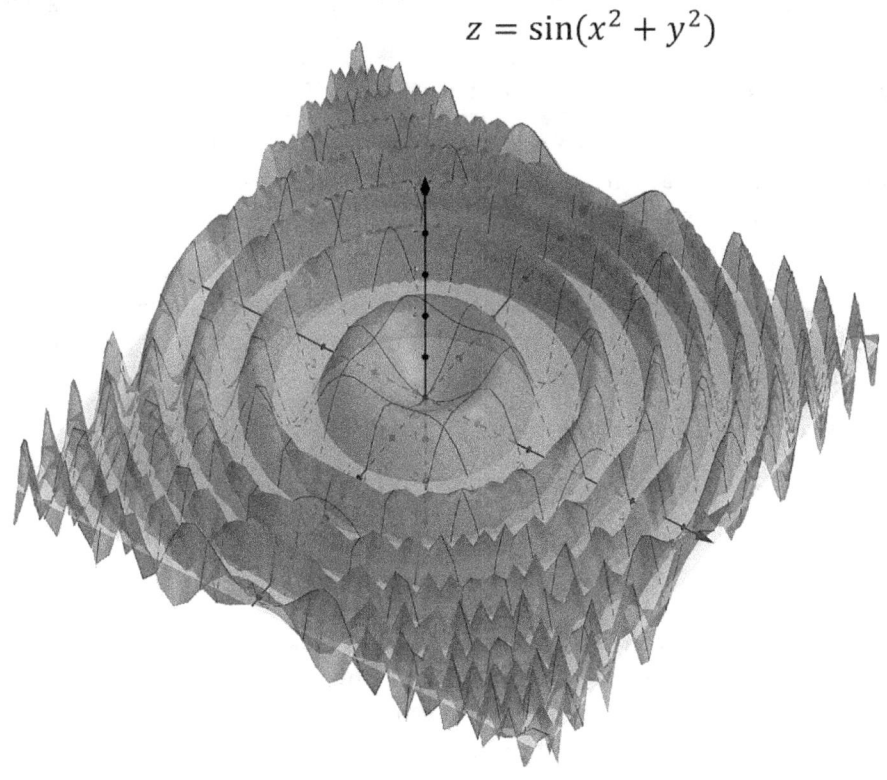

Figure 99. Sinusoidal surface resembling ripples in a pond

The following are some additional graphs that the reader may want to try on an online 3D graphing tool such as the "3D Calculator" on the Geogebra site:

- $z = xy + \sin(x^2 + y^2)$
- $z = \log(x^2 + y^2)$
- $z = \sin(xy) + \log(x + y)$
- $x^2 + y^2 + z^2 = 9$
- $\exp\left(-\sin\left(\sqrt{x^2 + y^2}\right)\right)$.

6.3   Geodesic Polyhedrons and Geodesic Domes

In this subsection, we discuss 3-dimensional objects which are artful in and of themselves, but which are also used in works of art such as geodesic domes. These objects are known generically as geodesic polyhedrons.

The Wikipedia article on geodesic polyhedron [73] provides the following definition:

> A **geodesic polyhedron** is a convex polyhedron made from triangles. They usually have icosahedral symmetry, such that they have 6 triangles at a vertex, except 12 vertices which have 5 triangles. They are the dual of corresponding Goldberg polyhedrons with mostly hexagonal faces.

Let's break this down into understandable pieces:

- First off, a **polyhedron** is simply a geometric object with flat polygonal faces. A **polygon** is a 2-dimensional object made from a finite number of line segments, e.g., triangles and hexagons are polygons.

- Convex means that if one selects any two points on the surface of an object, the line connecting the two points is completely within the interior of the object. In simple terms, a 3-dimensional convex object does not have any dents going inward (not mathematically precise but hopefully gives the general idea).

Figure 100 shows the construction of a geodesic polyhedron.

- The construction starts with an icosahedron (on the left).

- Each face of the icosahedron is divided into six triangles (2nd object from the left).

- Next, each triangle is again divided into 6 triangles.

- At this point (3rd object from the left), the object still has the same number of faces as the original icosahedron. We have only drawn lines on each face. In the final step, the vertices of each triangle are pushed out to meet the smallest sphere that encloses the original icosahedron. The object on the right is a geodesic polyhedron. To be clear, it is not a sphere but rather, a very close approximation.

Figures credits to Tom Ruen, see
https://commons.wikimedia.org/wiki/File:Geodesic_icosahedral_polyhedron_example2.png.

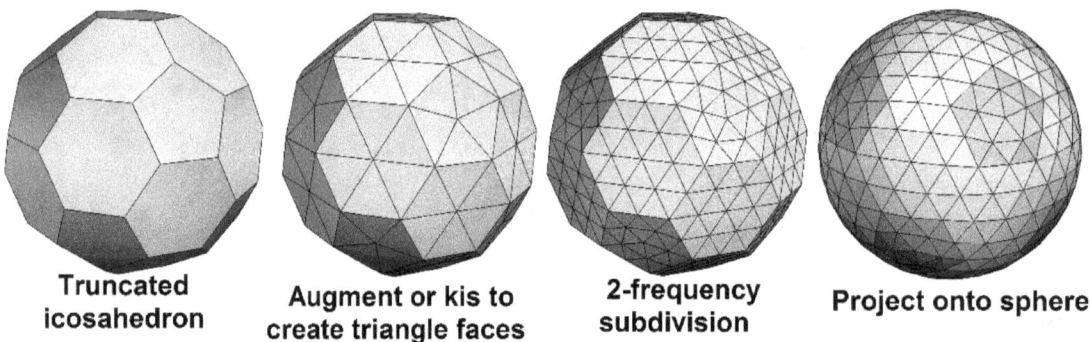

Truncated icosahedron   **Augment or kis to create triangle faces**   **2-frequency subdivision**   **Project onto sphere**

Figure 100. Construction of a geodesic polyhedron from an icosahedron

The Wikipedia article on geodesic polyhedrons [73] provides additional examples along with beautifully colored figures. The example constructions start with an icosahedron, an octahedron or a tetrahedron. This is followed by dividing each face into triangles (possible over several iterations). Finally, all the vertices are projected outward onto a sphere. As the number of triangles increases, the resulting geodesic polyhedron more closely approximates a sphere.

A geodesic dome is a spherical (or sometimes hemispherical) thin-shell structure based on a geodesic polyhedron. The triangular components of the dome are rigid and distribute the structural stress throughout the dome, thereby making geodesic domes able to withstand very heavy loads for their size.

The design of the first geodesic dome is credited to Walther Bauersfeld, chief engineer of the Carl Zeiss optical company, for a building to contain his planetarium (completed in 1923). Although Bauersfeld's dome could support a full skin of concrete, it was not until 1949 that R. Buckminster Fuller designed (and had built) a geodesic dome that could sustain its own weight. Fuller is credited with the popularization of geodesic domes.

Figure 101 shows the geodesic dome at the World of Science in Vancouver, BC (Canada).

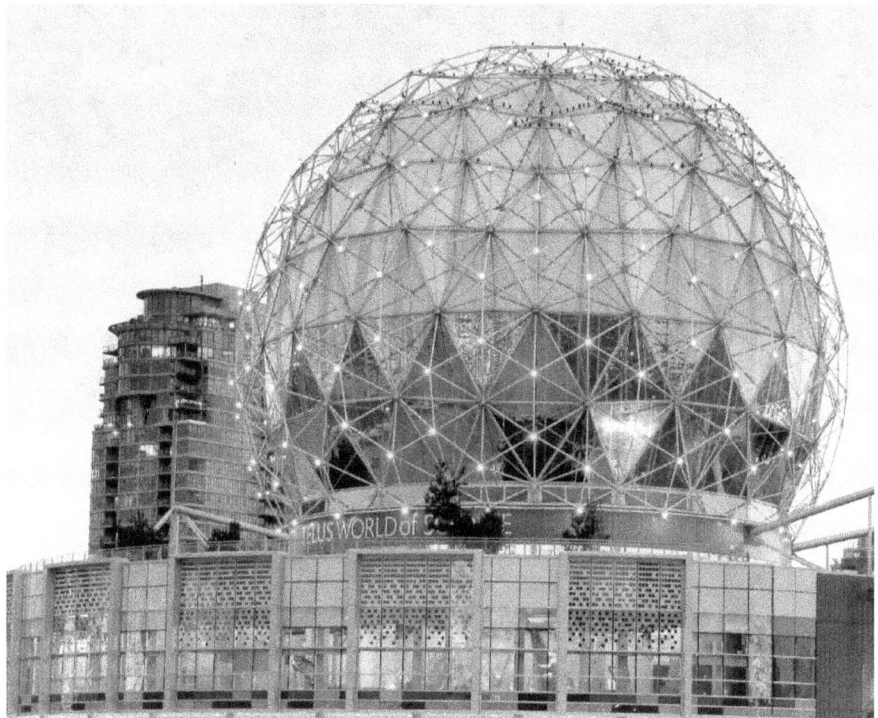

Figure 101. Geodesic dome at World of Science in Vancouver

6.4   Number Sequences

Number sequences, at least for the mathematically initiated, can have a certain beauty and even for the uninitiated, the graphical representation of some number sequence can be aesthetically pleasing.

6.4.1   Spirals Generated from Number Sequences

Consider the famous Fibonacci sequence

$$1, 1, 2, 3, 5, 8, 13, 21, 34, 55, 89, 144, \ldots$$

After the first two numbers in the sequence, each number is the sum of the previous two. The Fibonacci numbers can be converted to a winding sequence of squares with a quarter circle imposed on each square to form what is known as the Fibonacci spiral (see Figure 102).

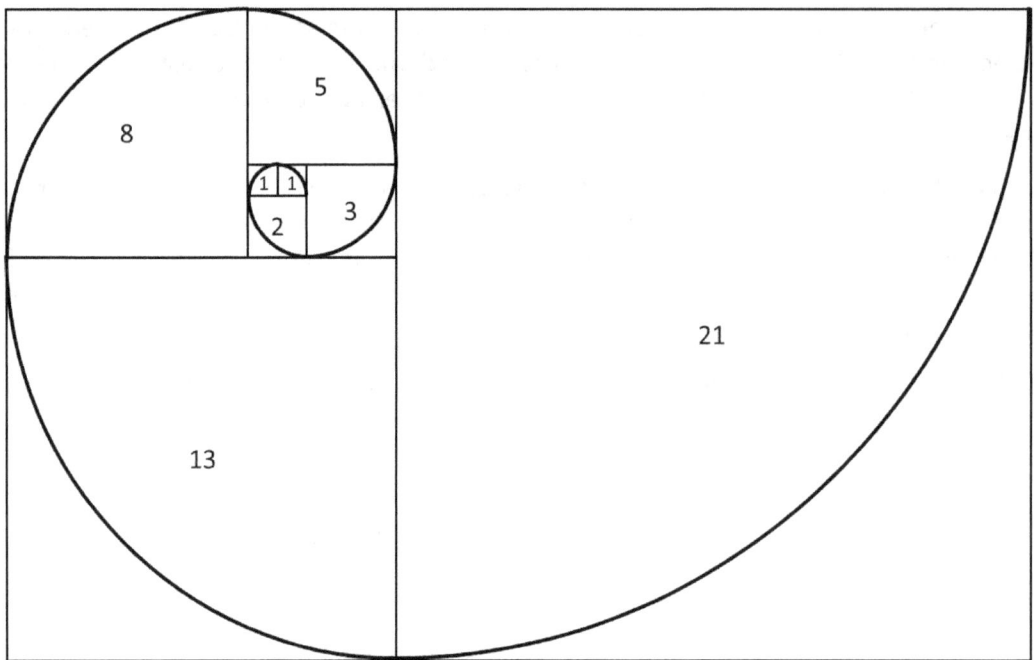

Figure 102. Fibonacci spiral

This approach lends itself to other sequences. Consider the sequence of powers of 2 alternating with the number 1, i.e.,

$$1, 2, 1, 4, 1, 8, 1, 16, 1, 32, \ldots$$

The associated spiral is shown in Figure 103. Each quarter-circle of radius 1 effectively creates a sharp turn.

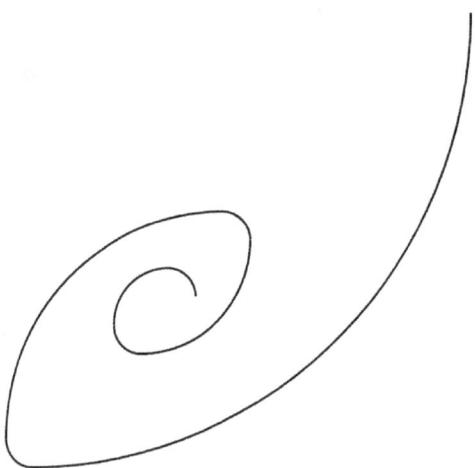

Figure 103. Spiral generated from powers of 2 alternating with the number 1

This technique can be used to generate pleasing figures from a finite sequence. Figure 104 was generated from the sequence 1,2,3,2,2,1,3 repeated four times. After four repetitions, the graph overlaps itself.

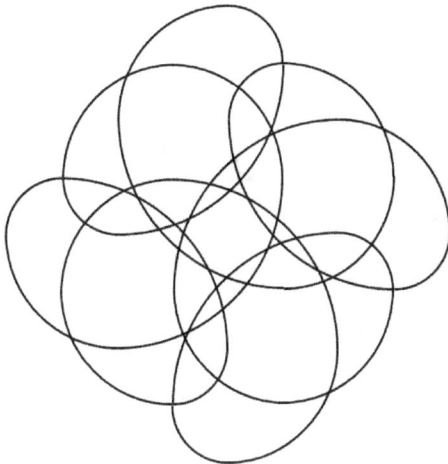

Figure 104. Spiral generated by a finite sequence

The reader may want to give a try in graphing the sequence $2, 1, 3, 1, 1, 2, 3$ (repeated four times). [**Author's Remark**: I drew the previous figures using Microsoft PowerPoint and the quarter circle shape.]

6.4.2   Polygonal Numbers

A **polygonal number** is a number represented as dots arranged in the shape of a regular polygon. Polygonal numbers give rise to associated sequences. For example, the numbers in the sequence

$$1, 3, 6, 10, 15, 21, \ldots$$

are known as the triangular numbers and can be represented pictorially as shown in Figure 105.

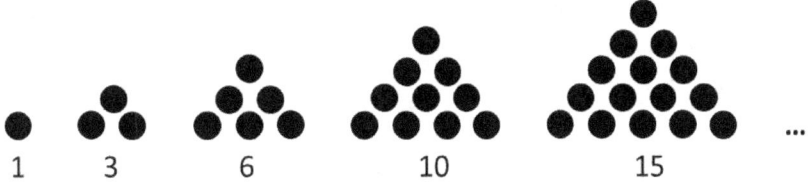

Figure 105. Sequence of triangular numbers

There are also square, pentagonal, hexagonal and in general, "n-agonal" numbers, and associated sequences and diagrams. The rule for enlarging the polygon to the next size is to extend two adjacent edges by one point and to then add the required extra sides between those points. This leads to a perfect regular lattice for square numbers (see Figure 106) but not for higher order polygons such as pentagons (see Figure 107).

Credits for Figure 106 and Figure 107 go to Aldo Aldoz, see the Wikipedia article on polygonal numbers [74].

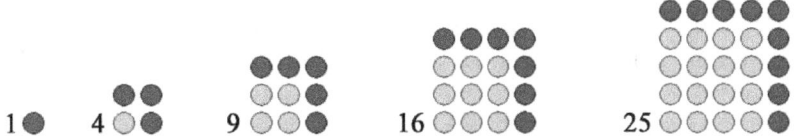

Figure 106. Sequence formed by square numbers

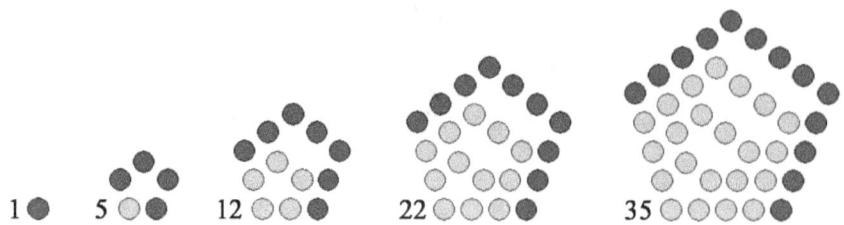

Figure 107. Sequence formed by pentagonal numbers

There is a closed form for the nth term in a polygonal sequence where the polygons have s sides, i.e.,

$$P(s,n) = (s-2)\frac{n(n-1)}{2} + n$$

For example, the 6th term in the pentagonal number sequence is $P(5,6) = (5-2)\frac{6(5)}{2} + 6 = 51$.

By the way, an extensive repository of number sequences is available at the On-Line Encyclopedia of Integer Sequences, see http://oeis.org. For example, try typing the sequence $1, 5, 12, 22, 35, 51$ in the search box and the OEIS site will identify this as the pentagonal number sequence and return a large list of references with additional information.

6.4.3   Pascal's Triangle

Pascal's triangle is an array of finite sequences (see Figure 108). Each row is constructed from the previous row. For example, the bold number 10 in 5th row is the sum of the two numbers directly above it to the left and right (also shown in bold). (Note that the rows are counted starting with 0, e.g., the sequence "1 2 1" is in row 2.)

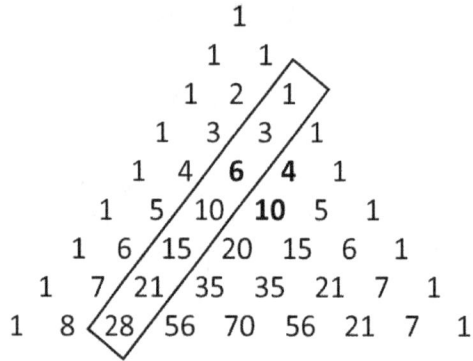

Figure 108. Pascal's triangle

As noted in the Wikipedia article on the topic [75]:

> In much of the Western world, it is named after the French mathematician Blaise Pascal, although other mathematicians studied it centuries before him in India, Persia (Iran), China, Germany, and Italy.

> The pattern of numbers that forms Pascal's triangle was known well before Pascal's time. Pascal innovated many previously unattested uses of the triangle's numbers, uses he

described comprehensively in the earliest known mathematical treatise to be specially devoted to the triangle, his Traité du triangle arithmétique (1654; published 1665). Centuries before, discussion of the numbers had arisen in the context of Indian studies of combinatorics and of binomial numbers, and the Greeks' study of figurate numbers.

One of the more direct motivations for Pascal's triangle comes from the raising of powers of terms of the form $(x + y)$. Consider the following:

$$(x + y)^2 = 1 \cdot x^2 + 2xy + 1 \cdot y^2$$

$$(x + y)^3 = 1 \cdot x^3 + 3x^2y + 3xy^2 + 1 \cdot y^3$$

$$(x + y)^4 = 1 \cdot x^4 + 4x^3y + 6x^2y^2 + 4xy^3 + 1 \cdot y^4$$

In fact, the correspondence between the coefficients in the expansion of $(x + y)^n$ holds for all positive integer values of n.

There are many other patterns associated with Pascal's triangle, e.g., the numbers in the rectangle in Figure 108 are the triangular numbers that we discussed in the previous subsection.

An example of the so-called Hockey Stick Pattern is shown Figure 109. The sum of the numbers in the "stick" rectangle equals the number in the "blade" just below. In the example suggested in the figure, we have that

$$1 + 4 + 10 + 20 + 35 + 56 + 84 = 210$$

Pascal's triangle is rotated 45 degrees counterclockwise in this example.

1	1	1	1	1	1	1	1	1	1	1
1	2	3	4	5	6	7	8	9	10	
1	3	6	10	15	21	28	36	45		
1	4	10	20	35	56	84	120			
1	5	15	35	70	126	210				
1	6	21	56	126	252					
1	7	28	84	210						
1	8	36	120							
1	9	45								
1	10									
1										

Figure 109. Hockey stick pattern

For a discussion of many more patterns related to Pascal's triangle, see the article "Patterns in Pascal's Triangle" [76] at the "Cut the Knot" website.

6.4.4   Lazy Caterer's Sequence

The sequence $1, 2, 4, 7, 11, 16, 22, 29, 37, 46, 56, 67, 79, \ldots$ is pretty easy to figure, i.e., the difference between two successive numbers is increased by 1 at each step. The associated physical problem, however, is more interesting. Given a pizza, cake, pie or some other circular object, in how many pieces can the object be divided with n cuts? The pieces do not need to be the same size.

The first 8 cases are shown in Figure 110. The number of pieces corresponds to the sequence noted above. Even at 8 slices, the diagram becomes very intricate and some of the pieces are very small – not a nice way to slice a pizza, cake or pie.

Figure credit to Gilles Castel, as presented in a response to a question on Quora, see https://www.quora.com/Is-there-a-name-for-this-mathematical-sequence-1-2-4-7-11-16-22-29-37-46-56.

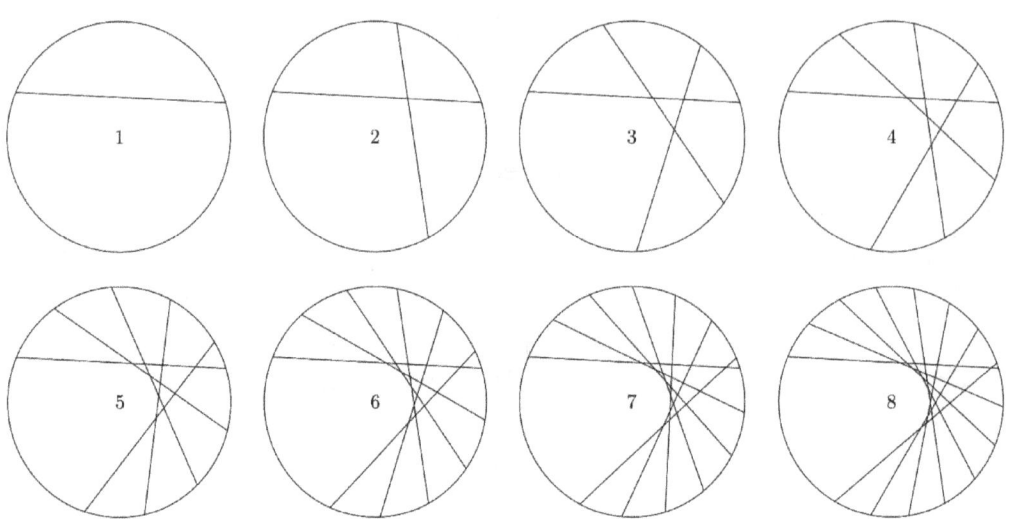

Figure 110. Lazy Caterer's sequence

The Lazy Caterer's sequence is cataloged as A000124 in the On-Line Encyclopedia of Integer Sequences, see http://oeis.org/A000124.

6.5   Voronoi Diagrams

A **Voronoi diagram** (named after Russian mathematician Georgy Voronoy) is a tiling of the plane based on a finite set of points S. Each point x in S is placed within a tile such that other points in the tile are closer to x than any other point in S. Figure 111 depicts the Voronoi diagram corresponding to the set

$S = \{A,B,C,D,E,F,G,H,I,J,K,L,M\}$

The tiles on the boundary of the figure (i.e., the tiles surrounding A, B, J, K, L, M, F and G) are infinite. The figure was created using the Voronoi function at GeoGebra (see https://www.geogebra.org and the brief explanation at https://youtu.be/41LFloW4VHQ).

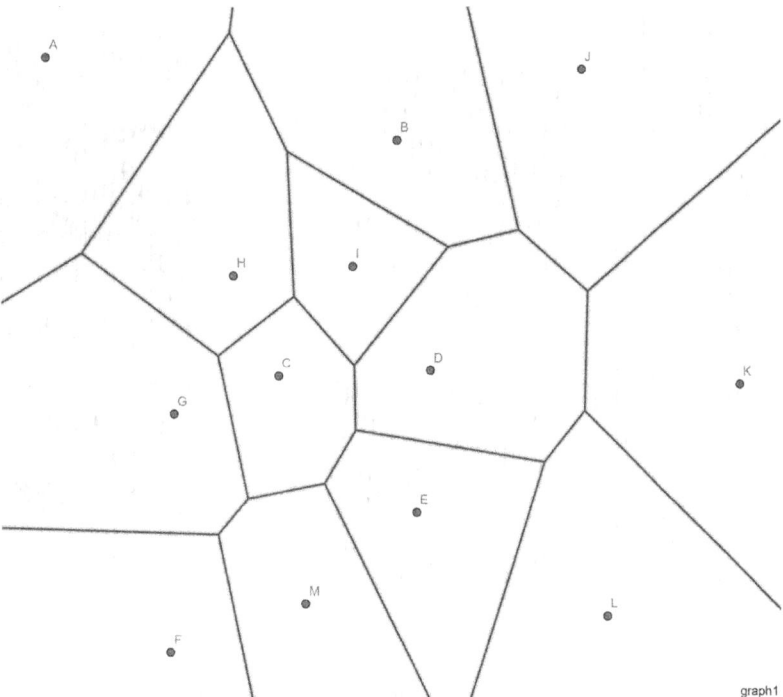

Figure 111. Example Voronoi diagram

Many generalizations are possible, e.g.,

- The simple case uses the Euclidean measure of distance between two points $A(x_1, y_1)$ and $B(x_2, y_2)$, i.e., $d(A,B) = \sqrt{(x_1 - x_2)^2 + (y_1 - y_2)^2}$. Alternately, one could use what is called the Manhattan (or street) distance given by $d(A,B) = |x_1 - x_2| + |y_1 - y_2|$. Further, measures other than distance can be used, e.g., the length of time it takes to travel to a given point.

- As noted in the Wikipedia article on Voronoi diagrams [77]: "Although a normal Voronoi cell is defined as the set of points closest to a single point in S, an nth-order Voronoi cell is defined as the set of points having a particular set of n points in S as its n nearest neighbors. Higher-order Voronoi diagrams also subdivide space."

- The concept can be generalized to 3 and higher dimensions.

6.6   Moiré Patterns

A **Moiré pattern** is formed by the interference produced when an opaque ruled pattern with transparent gaps is overlaid on a (usually) identical pattern. For the interference pattern to emerge, the overlapping patterns must be transposed, rotated, or be oriented at a slightly different angle.

In Figure 112, the Moiré pattern on the right is formed by overlapping the two patterns on the left.

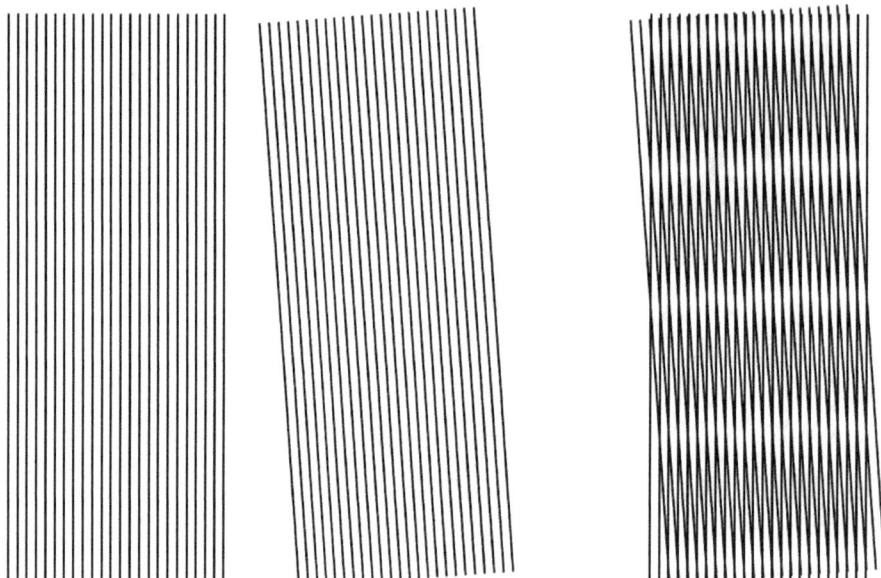

Figure 112. Moiré pattern formed by two overlapping array of straight lines

By varying the orientation of the overlap (via rotation or transposition), one can generate different Moiré patterns. Figure 113 shows two different patterns (middle and right) formed by varying the overlap of two copies of the figure on the left.

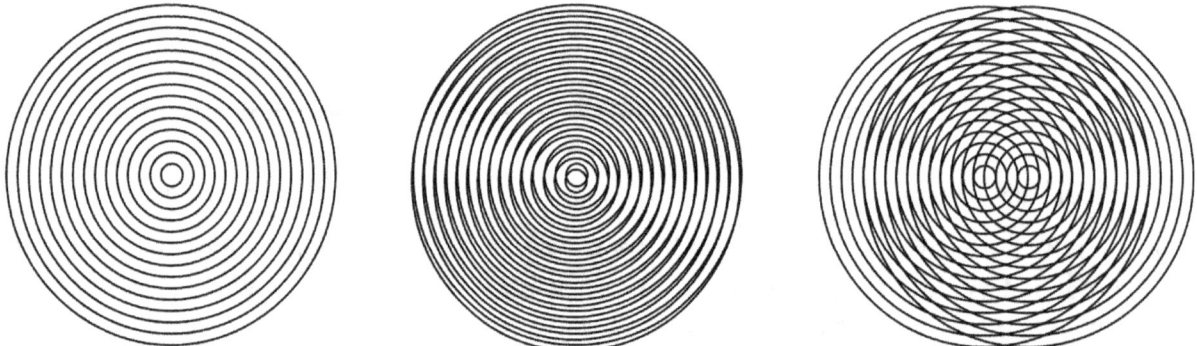

Figure 113. Moiré pattern formed by two overlapping sets of concentric circles

Figure 114 makes use of three overlapping copies of the set of concentric circles. [**Author's Remark**: This is my own design.]

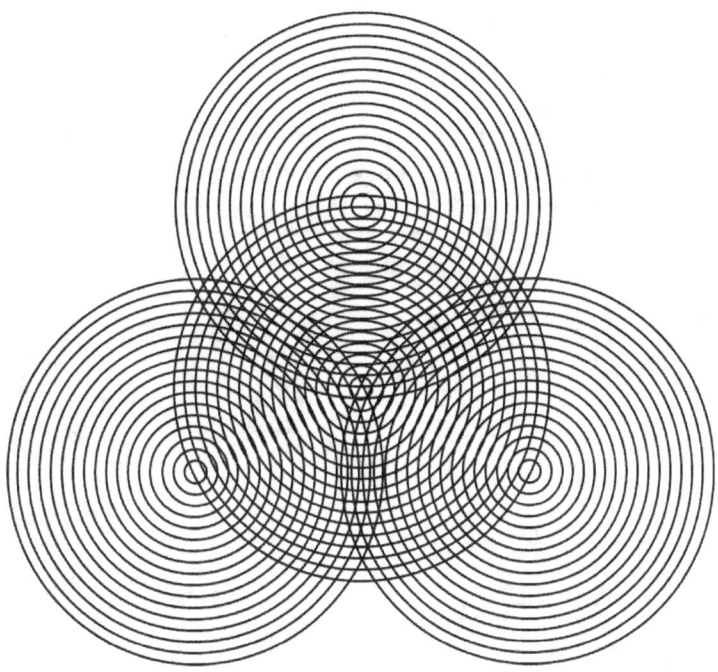

Figure 114. Moiré pattern formed by four overlapping sets of concentric circles

Victor Vasarely used Moiré patterns in the untitled work of art shown in Figure 115.

Figure credit: Masterworks Fine Art (MFA) Gallery, see
https://www.masterworksfineart.com/artists/victor-vasarely/multiple/untitled-3/id/w-3817.

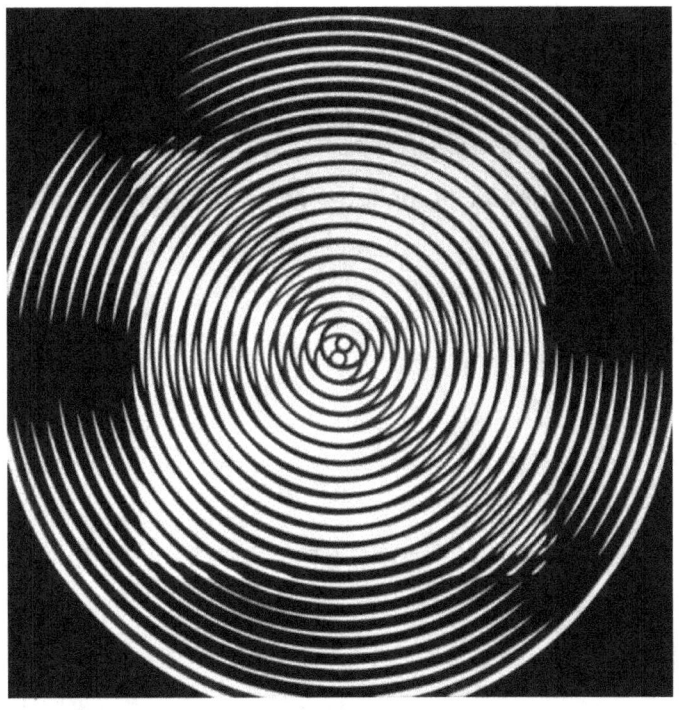

Figure 115. Victor Vasarely – Untitled

An unwanted Moiré pattern can present itself in a photograph when (for example) a grid pattern on the object being photographed conflicts with the sensor grid in the camera. In Figure 116, the pattern on the left represents the grid of a camera sensor and the pattern on the right is produced by an overlay of a pattern (on the object being photographed) of similar granularity to that of the camera sensor but slightly rotated (e.g., the weave pattern on an article of clothing). For a comprehensive discussion of this phenomena, see the article entitled "What is Moiré and How it Can Ruin Your Photos" [78].

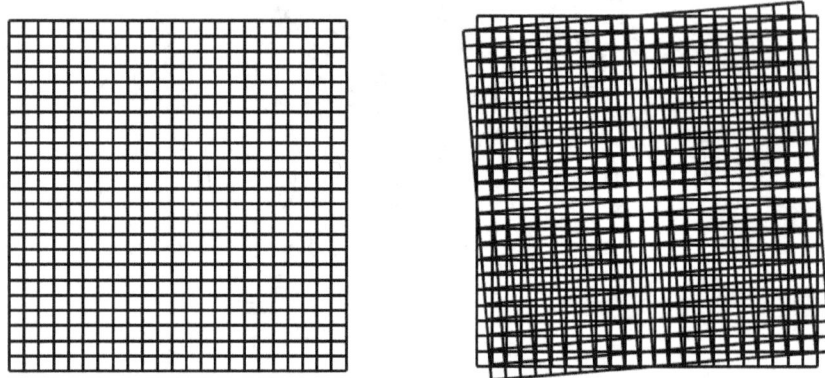

Figure 116. Moiré pattern formed by two overlapping

6.7   Golden Ratio

The **golden ratio** (also known as the golden mean, golden section, divine proportion, divine section, golden proportion, or golden number) is an irrational number used extensively in mathematics and art. Two positive numbers a and b are said to be in the golden ratio if the follow equality hold true:

$$\frac{a+b}{a} = \frac{a}{b}$$

If we let $\varphi = a/b$, we can solve for the golden ratio in the above equation.

Divide the numerator and denominator of the left-side of the above equation by b to get

$$\frac{\frac{a}{b}+1}{\frac{a}{b}} = a/b$$

which can be written as

$$\frac{\varphi+1}{\varphi} = \varphi$$

Using some algebra, we get the equation $\varphi^2 - \varphi - 1 = 0$. From the quadratic formula, we get the positive solution

$$\varphi = \frac{1+\sqrt{5}}{2} \cong 1.61803398875$$

In terms of photography, the golden ratio is sometimes used as an alternative to the **Rule of Thirds**. From the Wikipedia article "Rule of thirds" [79]:

The rule of thirds is a "rule of thumb" or guideline which applies to the process of composing visual images such as designs, films, paintings, and photographs. The guideline proposes that an image should be imagined as divided into nine equal parts by two equally spaced horizontal lines and two equally spaced vertical lines, and that important compositional elements should be placed along these lines or their intersections. Proponents of the technique claim that aligning a subject with these points creates more tension, energy and interest in the composition than simply centering the subject.

The photo of the Eiffel Tower in Figure 117 provides an example of the rule of thirds. Notice how the tower is placed along one of the grid lines (rather than dead center in the photo).

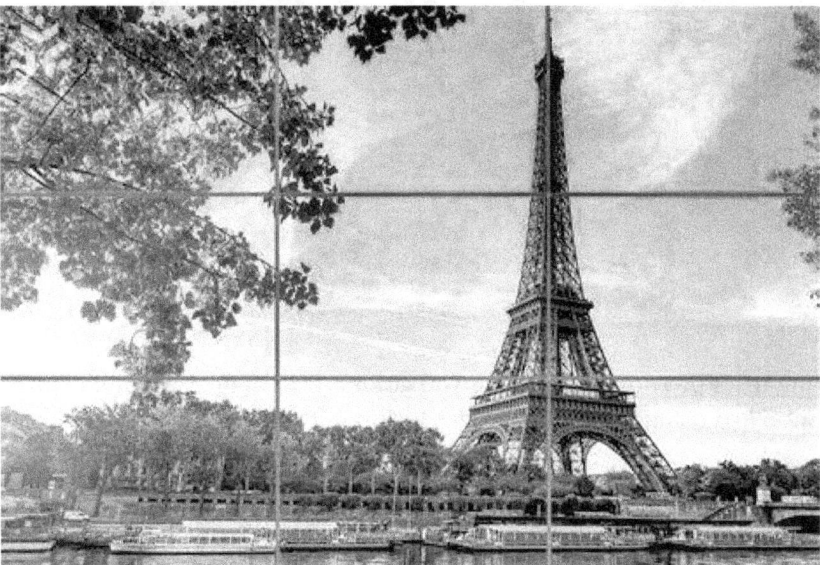

Figure 117. Example of the "rule of thirds"

In a variation of the rule of thirds, the grid is based on the proportions of the golden ratio. The grid in Figure 118 is based on the golden ratio. The row and column widths are in the proportion 1.618 : 1 : 1.618.

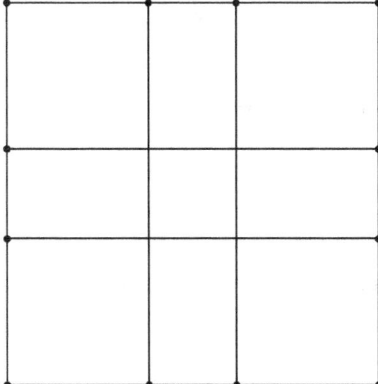

Figure 118. Variation of rule of thirds based on the Golden Ratio

Figure 119 depicts a photo of a temple that has been cropped to fit the golden ratio grid. We will return to this photo in Section 7.4 concerning fractals.

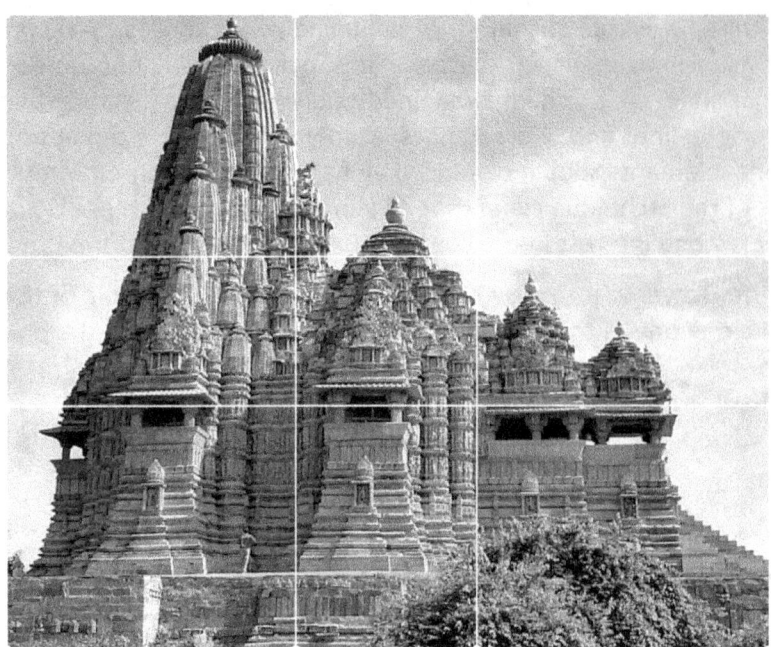

Figure 119. Photo cropped to fit the golden ratio grid

Some photo editing tools provide support for the golden ratio. For example, Figure 119 was edited with Corel PaintShop Pro using the golden ratio option in the cropping tool.

The Fibonacci spiral is yet another way to use the golden ratio in art. Recall from Section 6.4.1 that the Fibonacci numbers are a sequence of numbers formed by a simple recursive formula. It turns out that the ratio of successive Fibonacci numbers converges to the golden ratio, see Table 1.

Table 1. Ratio of successive Fibonacci numbers

1/1	2/1	3/2	5/3	8/5	13/8	21/13	34/21	55/34	89/55	144/89
1	2	1.5	1.6667	1.6	1.625	1.615385	1.619048	1.617647059	1.618181818	1.617977528

The idea is to use the Fibonacci spiral as a guide in architecture, paintings and photography. Some examples:

- Photographer Ansel Adams made extensive use of the Fibonacci spiral in his work [80].

- The Wikipedia article entitled "List of works designed with the golden ratio" [81] covers many paintings and works of architecture that are either based on or inspired by the golden ratio.

- The article "Importance of Golden Ratio in Architecture" [82] provides an overview of the use of the golden ratio in architecture.

Figure 120 is a grayscale version of a painting from cubist Armando Barrios with the Fibonacci spiral superimposed over the painting (of course not part of the original painting). Barrios uses mathematical shapes (such as spirals) in much of his artwork. For example, see his clock and mural in La Plaza del Rectorado at Ciudad Universitaria de Caracas in Venezuela (https://en.wikipedia.org/wiki/File:Clock-Armando_Barrios_UCV.JPG). Parts of various colored spirals appear throughout the mural.

[**Author's Remark**: Not convinced? Well, I'm not 100% sold on this either but keep in mind that it is unrealistic to expect artists to use complex shapes exactly as-is. The Fibonacci spiral serves more as an inspiration for composition in photography, painting, drawing and architecture.]

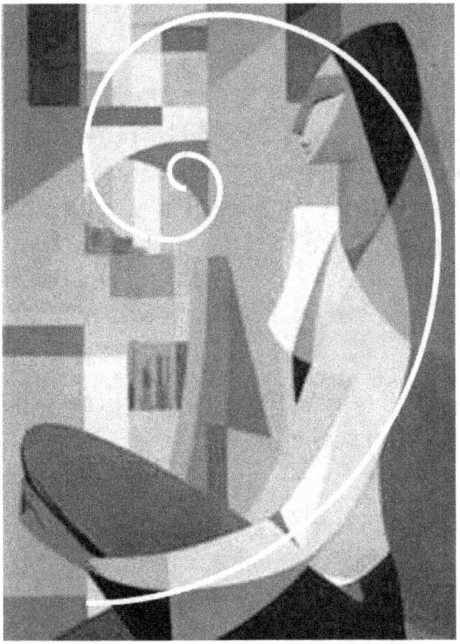

Figure 120. Painting by Armando Barrios fit to the Fibonacci spiral

7 Fractals

7.1 Overview

The Fractal Foundation defines **fractals** as follows:

> A fractal is a never-ending pattern. Fractals are infinitely complex patterns that are self-similar across different scales. They are created by repeating a simple process over and over in an ongoing feedback loop. Driven by recursion, fractals are images of dynamic systems – the pictures of Chaos. Geometrically, they exist in between our familiar dimensions. Fractal patterns are extremely familiar, since nature is full of fractals. For instance: trees, rivers, coastlines, mountains, clouds, seashells, hurricanes, etc. Abstract fractals – such as the Mandelbrot Set – can be generated by a computer calculating a simple equation over and over.

In the above definition, the examples in nature are only approximations to abstract fractals which repeat infinitely at smaller and smaller scales.

As an initial example, Figure 121 depicts the first few iterations of Sierpinski's triangle. Starting with a solid triangle (on the left), a triangle ¼ of the size of the original is removed (2nd from left). For the remaining three smaller triangles, do the same and continue the process indefinitely. At any step, if one focuses on just one of the black triangles, its interior appears no different from the original triangle. This is an example of self-similarity.

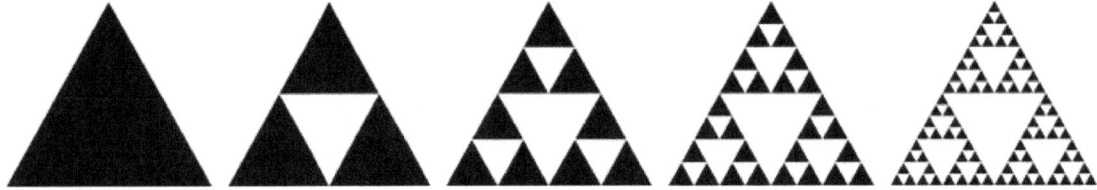

Figure 121. First few iterations of Sierpinski's triangle

Another common example of a fractal is the Koch snowflake (named after Swedish mathematician Helge von Koch). The starting point for the generation of the Koch snowflake is an equilateral triangle. At the first iteration, the middle third of each side of the triangle is replaced by two segments of $\frac{1}{3}$ length. After the first iteration, the figure has 12 sides, see Figure 122 (the dashed lines show what has been removed or are not part of the figure).

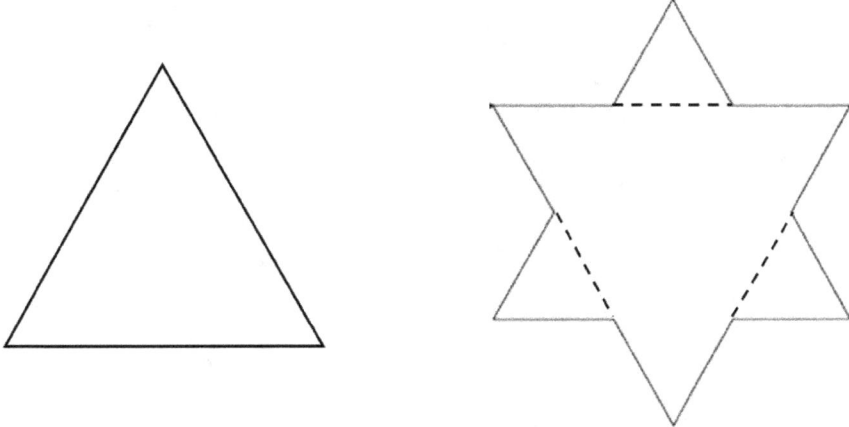

Figure 122. Koch snowflake – starting figure and first iteration

For each of the 12 sides of the polygon on the right of Figure 122, we repeat the process of removing the middle third and replacing it with 2 sides of $\frac{1}{3}$ length. This brings us to the polygon in Figure 123.

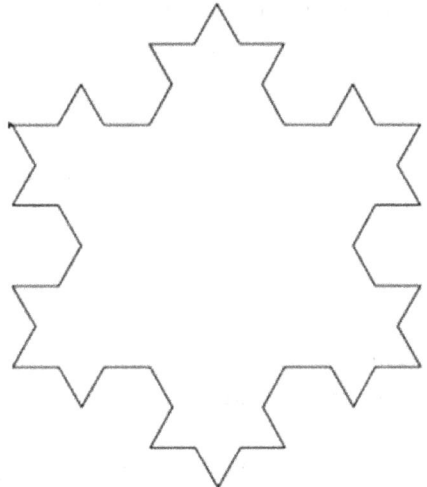

Figure 123. Koch snowflake after 2nd iteration

Repeating the process again, we start to get something that more closely resembles a snowflake (see Figure 124). The process continues indefinitely.

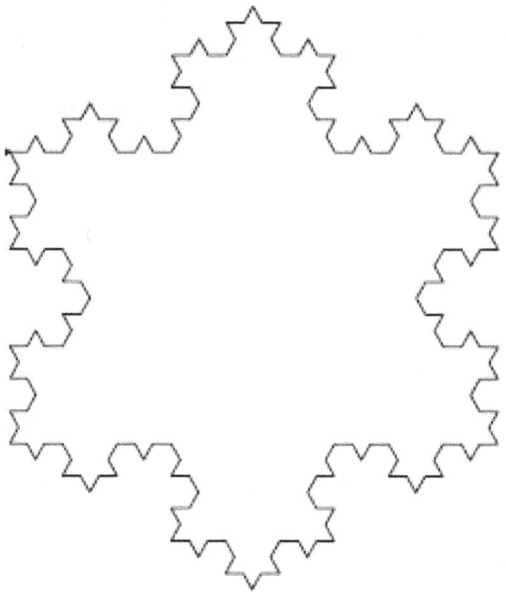

Figure 124. Koch snowflake after 3ʳᵈ iteration

The Python code used to generate the previous figures is provided below. In the function call (3ʳᵈ line from the end), the number in bold is the number of iterations. A value of 6 or more for the number iterations will take a very long time to complete. Even for a value of 5, the program takes about 10 minutes to complete (of course, this depends on the processing power of your computer).

```
import turtle
def koch_curve(t, iterations, length, shortening_factor, angle):
  if iterations == 0:
    t.forward(length)
  else:
    iterations = iterations - 1
    length = length / shortening_factor
    koch_curve(t, iterations, length, shortening_factor, angle)
    t.left(angle)
    koch_curve(t, iterations, length, shortening_factor, angle)
    t.right(angle * 2)
    koch_curve(t, iterations, length, shortening_factor, angle)
    t.left(angle)
    koch_curve(t, iterations, length, shortening_factor, angle)
t = turtle.Turtle()
t.hideturtle()
for i in range(3):
  koch_curve(t, 3, 300, 3, 60)
  t.right(120)
turtle.mainloop()
```

It is possible to tile the plane using Koch snowflakes of two different sizes (as shown in Figure 125).

Figure credits go to David Eppstein, see
https://commons.wikimedia.org/wiki/File:Koch_similarity_tiling.svg.

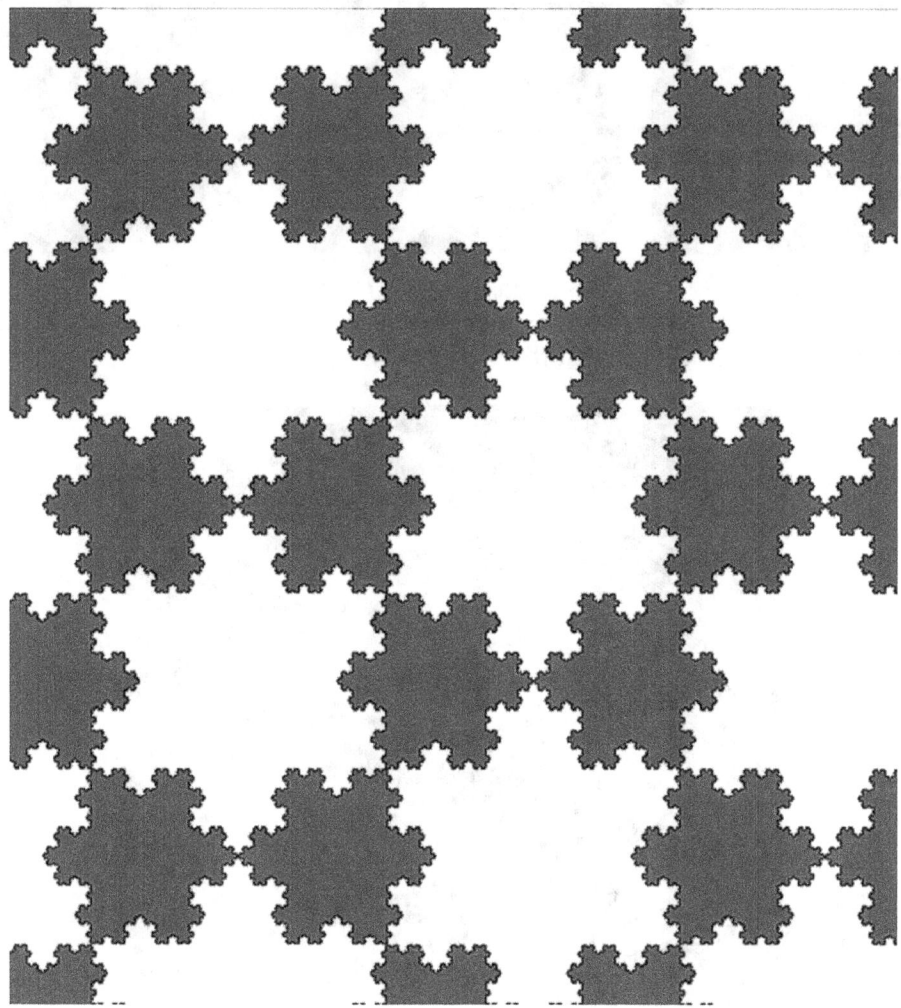

Figure 125. Tiling using Koch snowflakes of two different sizes

Some additional tilings that make use of fractals can be found in the article "Koch tiles" [83].

. . .

Fractals can also be constructed in 3 dimensions. Figure 126 shows the first three iterations of the Sierpinski pyramid (or tetrahedron). The Sierpinski pyramid is a three-dimensional analogue of the Sierpinski triangle, formed by repeatedly shrinking a four-sided pyramid to ½ its original height, placing together four copies of reduced pyramid with corners touching, and then repeating the process.

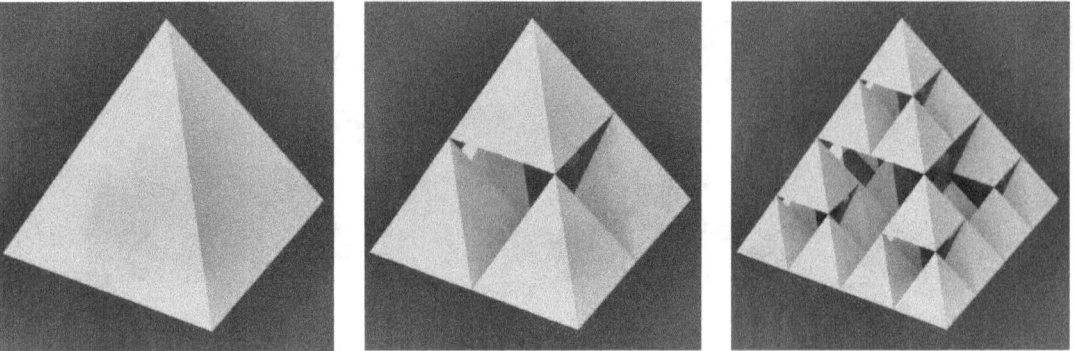

Figure 126. First three iterations of the Sierpinski pyramid

Figure 127 shows the Sierpinski pyramid after 7 iterations.

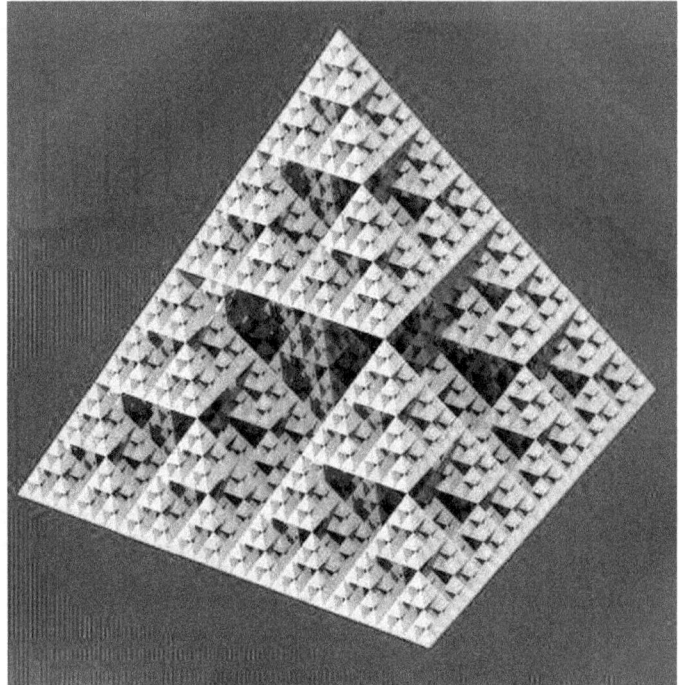

Figure 127. Sierpinski pyramid after 7 iterations

Figure 126 and Figure 127 were derived from an animated gif, with credits to Datumizer (see https://commons.wikimedia.org/wiki/File:Sierpinski_pyramid_a.gif).

7.2 Terminology

7.2.1 Self-similarity

A key characteristic of fractals is self-similarity. We've seen examples of self-similarity in the Sierpinski triangle and the Koch snowflake. Dictionary.com provides the following definition of **self-similarity**:

> The property of having a substructure analogous or identical to an overall structure. For example, a part of a line segment is itself a line segment, and thus a line segment exhibits

self-similarity. By contrast, no part of a circle is a circle, and thus a circle does not exhibit self-similarity. Fractals such the Sierpinski triangle are self-similar to an arbitrary level of magnification; many natural phenomena, such as clouds and plants, are self-similar to some degree.

Not all fractals are self-similar, and vice versa (e.g., a line is self-similar but is not a fractal). The Mandelbrot set is often cited as an example of a quasi-similar fractal, i.e., the pattern is only approximated as one zooms-in on the figure. For a good introduction to the Mandelbrot Set, see the YouTube video "The Mandelbrot Set: How it Works, and Why it's Amazing!" [84].

The Mandelbrot set is shown in Figure 128.

Figure 128. Mandelbrot set

Figure 129 depicts a multi-level zoom into the Mandelbrot set. Notice that something similar to, but not exactly the same as, the original outer diagram appears several times.

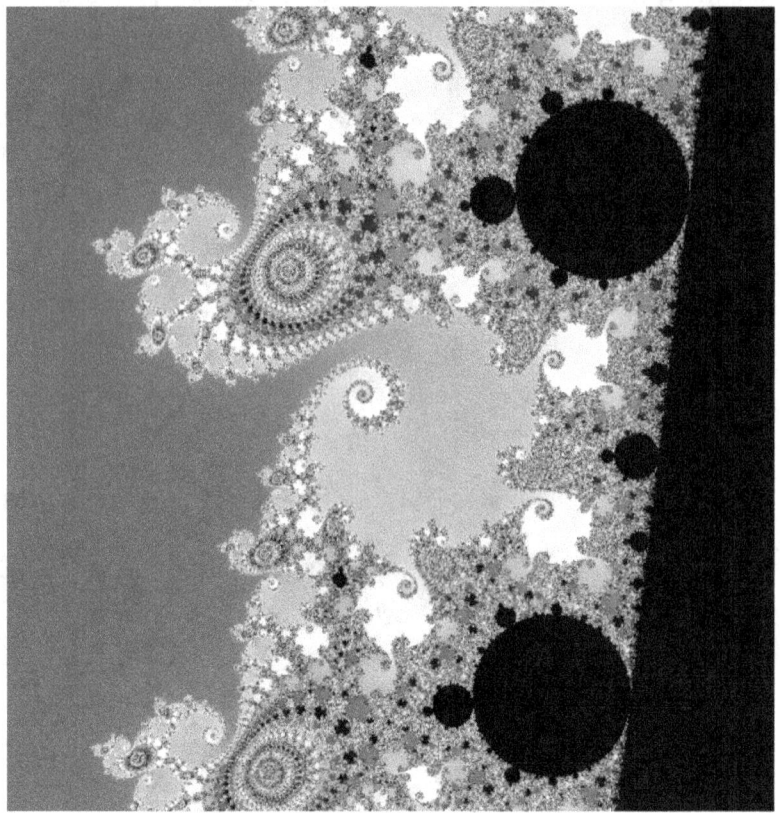

Figure 129. Zoom down several levels into the Mandelbrot set

Figure 128 and Figure 129 were created using the "Explore the Mandelbrot Set" applet from David Eck at http://math.hws.edu/eck/js/mandelbrot/MB.html.

7.2.2   Fractal Dimension

From Euclidean geometry, we know that a point is of 0 dimension, a line is of dimension 1, a plane is of dimension 2 and the space in which we live (the universe) is of 3 spatial dimensions. Fractals have fractional dimensions. In order to see how the dimension of a fractal is computed, we start with an analysis of "normal" objects that have whole number dimensions.

In Figure 130, consider the first row which shows a line of unit length on the left and then two lines of ½ unit length. When a line is reduced by ½, $2 = 2^1$ segments are required to equal the length of the original line. We can do the same game with a square (second row of the figure). If we reduce the length of a side by ½, then it takes $4 = 2^2$ smaller squares to equal the original square. Further, there is nothing special about ½ reduction. If we reduced the length of a side to 1/k of the original, then it would take k^2 smaller squares to equal the area of the original square. Finally, we consider the cube in the third row. If we reduce the length of an edge by ½ then it takes 2^3 smaller cubes to equal the volume of the original cube.

The approach in the above examples leads one to a pattern, i.e., the number of pieces (call it N) after a reduction (call it $\frac{1}{R}$) equals R^D where D is the dimension of the object. Thus, we have the following simple equation:

$$N = \frac{1}{\left(\frac{1}{R}\right)^D}$$

which can be rewritten as follow if one takes the log base 10 (or any other base for that matter) on both sides of the equation:

$$D = \frac{\log_{10} N}{\log_{10} R}$$

This is known as the Hausdorff–Besicovitch dimension (sometimes referred to as just the **Hausdorff dimension**).

If we take the cube example, then $N = 2^3$ and $R = 2$ which gives us $D = \frac{\log_{10} 2^3}{\log_{10} 2} = \frac{3\log_{10} 2}{\log_{10} 2} = 3$ which is as expected – no surprise here. However, the point of this exercise is to apply the same equation to fractals! In the bottom row of Figure 130, the first iteration of one side of the Koch snowflake is shown. In this case, $R = 3$ and $N = 4$ which implies the dimension of the Koch snowflake is

$$D = \frac{\log_{10} 4}{\log_{10} 3} \cong 1.26186$$

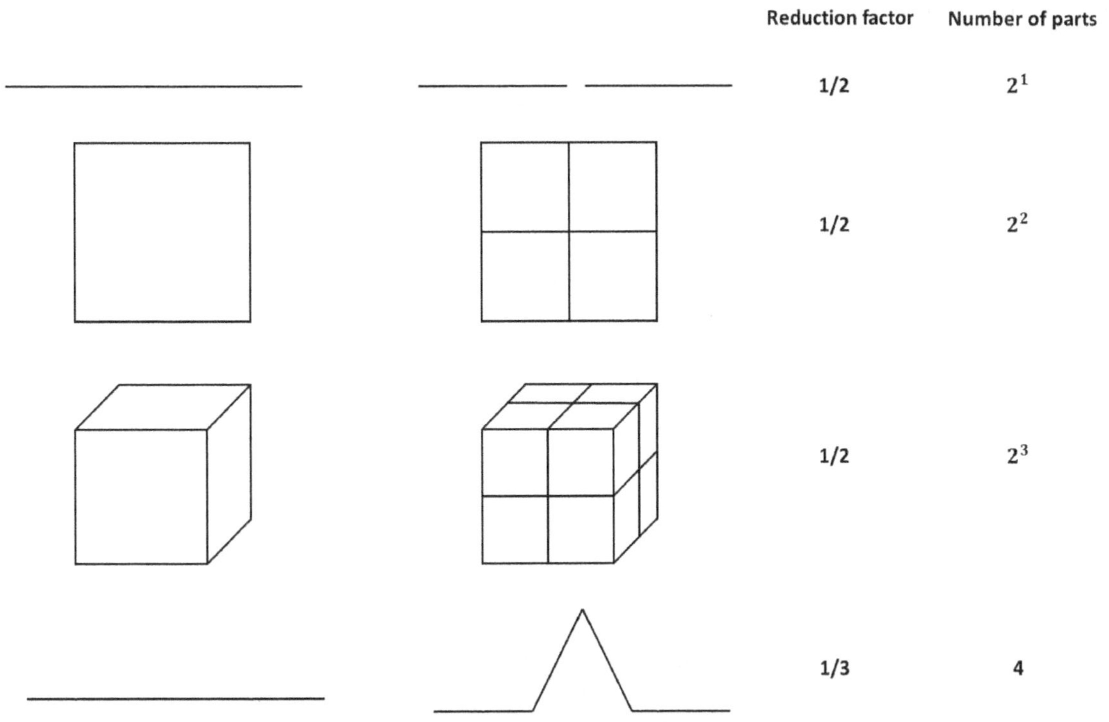

.

		Reduction factor	Number of parts
		1/2	2^1
		1/2	2^2
		1/2	2^3
		1/3	4

Figure 130. Analysis of dimension

An extensive list of the Hausdorff dimensions for fractals (both abstract and real) can be found at the Wikipedia article entitled "List of fractals by Hausdorff dimension" [85]. This article has a section entitled "Random and natural fractals" where estimates for the dimension of some real-world objects (as opposed to abstract mathematical objects) are provided. For example, the Hausdorff dimension of the coastline of England is estimated to be 1.25. While the coastline of Norway is even more extreme, it has an estimated Hausdorff dimension of 1.52. The idea is to measure the coastline at one level of granularity (e.g., yards) and then at a smaller level of granularity (e.g., feet). This provides sufficient information to calculate the Hausdorff dimension. The article also provides some interesting dimension estimates for surfaces, e.g., the surface of broccoli has an estimated Hausdorff dimension of 2.7 and the surface of a human lung has an estimated Hausdorff dimension of 2.97 (almost 3D and we are only talking about the surface of a lung).

7.2.3   Nowhere Differentiable

[**Author's Remark**: This subsection and the next are a bit more technical than other parts of this book, and admittedly, diverge from the theme of this book. However, I feel that a basic discussion of fractals would be incomplete without at least mentioning the concepts of nowhere differentiable and infinite perimeter, both of which are common to most fractals.]

A graph is **differentiable** at a given point if there is a unique tangent line at that point. A graph that is differentiable everywhere is sometimes referred to as being smooth. Many, but not all, fractals are just the opposite, i.e., nowhere differentiable.

For example, the parabola shown in Figure 131 is differentiable (i.e., has a unique tangent line) at every point. The figure also shows the unique tangent line at the point (2,4) on the parabola, see the dashed line in the figure.

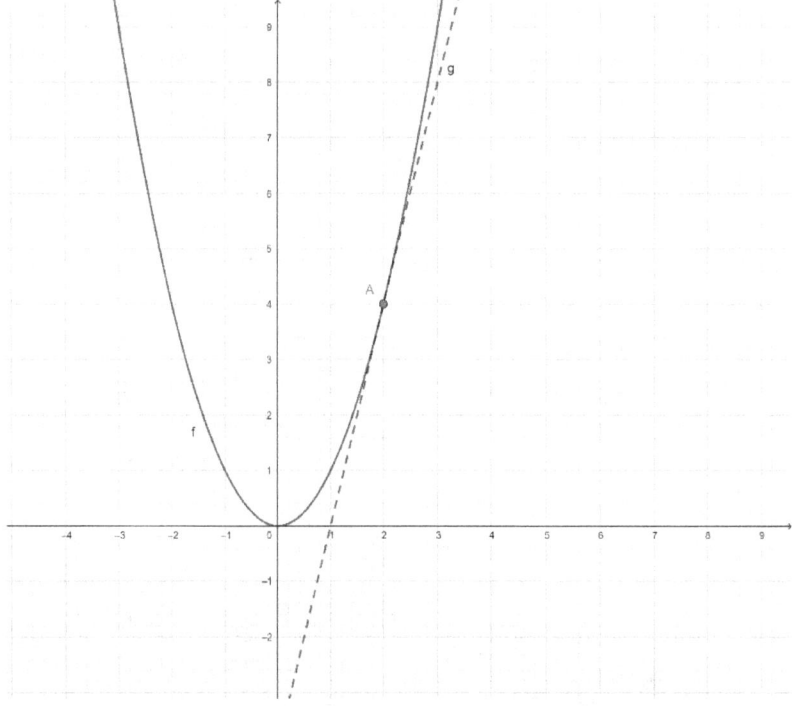

Figure 131. Parabola and tangent line at the point (2,4)

Figure 132 shows the graph of the absolute value of x (V-shaped graph) and two of an infinite number of tangent lines (dashed and dotted lines in the figure) at the point (0,0). At the point (0,0), the graph of the absolute value of x is not differentiable. However, at all other points, the graph of the absolute value of x is differentiable.

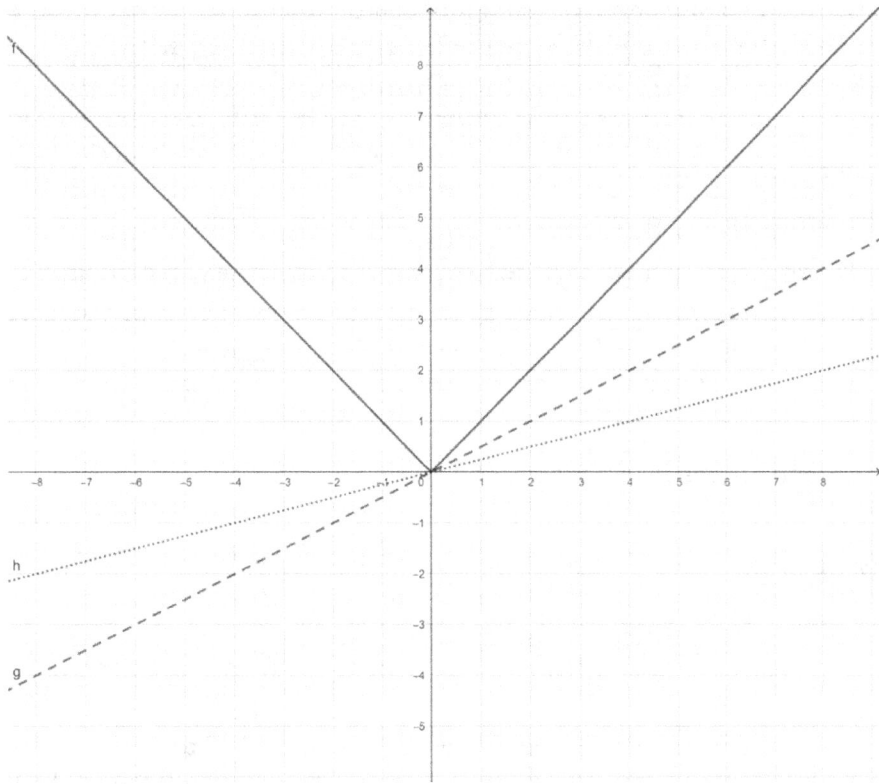

Figure 132. Graph of the absolute value of x

On the other hand, the graph of the Koch curve is non-differentiable at every point. At every point on the Koch curve, we have a "sharp corner" similar to the point (0,0) in the previous example concerning the absolute value of x.

The idea of a continuous function which is nowhere differentiable goes back to long before the fractal concept was popularized by Benoit Mandelbrot in 1975. In 1872, famous mathematician Karl Weierstrass published an example of a nowhere differentiable but everywhere continuous function. This function is essentially a fractal. The Wikipedia article entitled "Weierstrass function" [86] shows the Weierstrass function after several iterations and also provides an animation that emphasizes the point that the function is self-similar (i.e., looks the same at all levels of granularity). The description of the Weierstrass function is fairly complex which motivated Helge von Koch to construct an example (i.e., the Koch snowflake) with a simple construction method.

On the other hand, there are graphs which are considered to be fractals but which are differentiable almost everywhere. ("Almost everywhere" [87] is actually a precisely defined term in mathematics which means everywhere except on a set of measure zero.) The Cantor function [88] is an example of a fractal that has derivative 0 (i.e., tangle line with slope 0) almost everywhere.

Whether or not to include "nowhere differentiable" in the definition of fractals is a debatable point. An interesting discussion on the topic can be found on the Stack Exchange topic of mathematics under the title "Do all fractals have this property?" [89].

[**Author's Remark**: This type of discussion, concerning the classification of objects, occurs in many places in math, science and elsewhere. The point of contention usually centers around what characteristic or characteristics need to be present in order to place a particular object in a specific category. I've personally seen such discussions in my past work in telecommunications standards. The discussions can go on for years with no conclusion. My view is to just list the characteristics attributable to a given type of object and leave it at that, i.e., do not insist on classification.]

7.2.4   Infinite Perimeter

Many but not all 2-dimensional objects (considered to be fractals) have infinite perimeter. This would seem to be a natural assumption since at each iteration one increases the length of the fractal's perimeter. For example, the Koch snowflake (in fact, even just a portion of the Koch snowflake) has an infinite perimeter. To see this, consider an initial triangle with side of length s:

- After one iteration, the figure has length $3 \cdot s \cdot \dfrac{4}{3}$

- After two iterations, the figure has length $3 \cdot s \cdot \left(\dfrac{4}{3}\right)^2$

- The same pattern continues, and after n iterations, the length of the figure is $3 \cdot s \cdot \left(\dfrac{4}{3}\right)^n$.

Since $\dfrac{4}{3} > 1$, $\left(\dfrac{4}{3}\right)^n$ continues to increase without limit as n increase. As n approach infinity, so does the length of the figure. Interestingly, the area enclosed by the Koch snowflake is finite and given by the formula $\dfrac{2s^2\sqrt{3}}{5}$.

However, there are fractals (or at least what some would consider fractals) that have finite length. For example, the Cantor function [88] and the Minkowski question-mark function [90] both have length 2. In such cases, it is still true that the perimeter increases at each step, but the sum of the incremental increases in perimeter converges to a finite number.

7.3   Methods of Generating Fractals

There are several methods for generating fractals. We have already seen examples of the methods listed below:

- Iterated Function Systems (IFS) – uses fixed geometric replacement rules, e.g., Koch snowflake

- Finite subdivision rules – uses a recursive procedure for refinement of a tiling, e.g., the Sierpinski triangle.

- Escape-time fractals – uses a formula or recurrence relation at each point in a space (such as the complex plane). The Mandelbrot set is an example of this approach. The Mandelbrot set is the set of complex numbers c for which the function $f_c(z) = z^2 + 2$ does not diverge when iterated from $z = 0$, i.e., the set of complex numbers c such that

$f_c(0), f_c(f_c(0)), f_c(f_c(f_c(0))), \ldots$ remains bounded in absolute value. For an overview of the process that creates the Mandelbrot set, see the YouTube video entitled "The Mandelbrot Set - Numberphile" [91]. This video assumes a basic knowledge of complex numbers. For readers not familiar with complex numbers, see the Khan Academy video entitled Introduction to Complex Numbers [92].

In addition to the above approaches, there are also strange attractors, L-systems and random fractals.

An attractor is a set of numerical values towards which a system tends to evolve, under a wide range of initial values. System values that get close enough to the attractor values remain close even if slightly disturbed. Attractors that exhibit a fractal structure are referred to as **strange attractors**.

The **logistic map** is an example of a strange attractor. It is often noted as an example of how complex, chaotic behavior can arise from very simple non-linear dynamical equations. The logistic map models the growth of a population with the recurrence equation:
$x_{n+1} = rx_n(1 - x_n)$

The parameter x_n is the ratio (at time n) of the existing population to the maximum possible population that a given environment can support. The parameter r is the "driving parameter", i.e., drives population increase. When $r > 1$, r drives the population constantly higher; but as it does so, the "damping term" $1 - x_n$ becomes smaller and smaller, and in doing so, gradually becomes a counterbalance to the driving force of r.

In order to compute the population at all future times (i.e., for all values of n), we just need the value for r and for x_0. For $r \le 3$, the value of x_n will converge on a single value as n increases. For $3 < r \le 1 + \sqrt{6}$, x_n alternates between two values. As r increase beyond $1 + \sqrt{6}$, the graph becomes more complex, with x_n alternating between 4, 8 and more values. For most values of r beyond 3.56995, the logistic map exhibits chaotic behavior (i.e., with no oscillations of finite period). However, there are still certain isolated ranges of r (beyond 3.56995) that show non-chaotic behavior; these are sometimes called islands of stability. Figure 133 shows $x = \lim\limits_{n \to \infty} x_n$ plotted against r. The main point for the discussion here is that the graph of the logistic map is fractal. For example, if you zoom in on the top "branch" of Figure 133, it looks exactly the same as the entire graph.

Figure credits to Jordan Pierce, see
https://commons.wikimedia.org/wiki/File:Logistic_Bifurcation_map_High_Resolution.png.

For a more detailed description of the logistic map, see the Wikipedia article on the topic [93] and also the YouTube video entitled "This equation will change how you see the world (the logistic map)" [94].

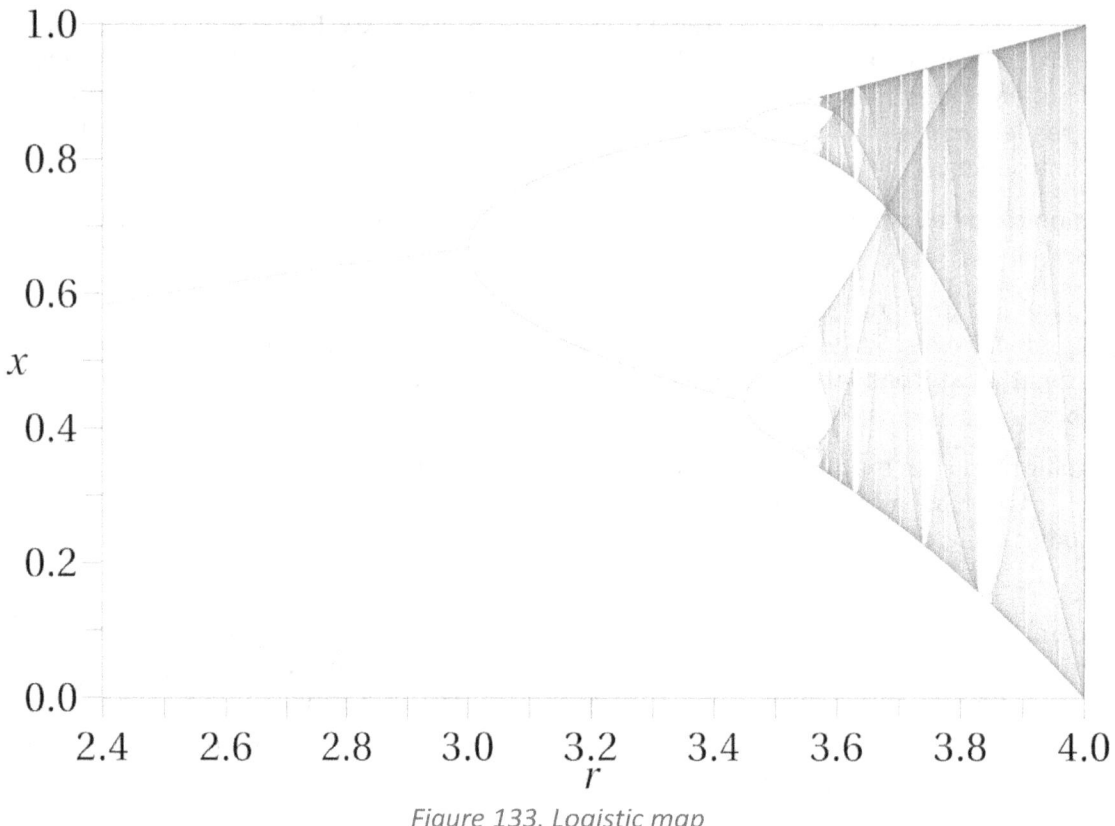

Figure 133. Logistic map

L-systems are used to construct various recursive structures. They are named after Aristid Lindenmayer, a Hungarian theoretical biologist and botanist, who used L-systems to describe the behavior of plant cells and to model the growth processes of plants [95]. However, L-systems have more general uses such as the generation of fractals. An L-system is a collection of symbols (e.g., letters from the alphabet), an initial set of symbols and a set of rules for modifying a string of symbols. A key point is that one can assign instructions to each symbol, e.g., "draw a line going to the left." The Wikipedia article on L-systems [96] provides several examples of how fractals can be generated with an L-systems. L-systems lend themselves to computer coding. The YouTube video entitled "L-Systems – The Nature of Code" [97] provides some examples of code used to generate fractals using L-systems.

All the methods for the generation of fractals discussed thus far have been deterministic in the sense that for a given starting arrangement, the same structure results. On the other hand, random fractals use stochastic rules (based on probability distributions) to generate structures. Random fractals generate different structures each time they are applied to the same starting arrangement. Fractal landscapes are examples of random fractals. From the Wikipedia article on fractal landscapes [100]:

> A fractal landscape is a surface generated using a stochastic algorithm designed to produce fractal behavior that mimics the appearance of natural terrain. In other words, the result of the procedure is not a deterministic fractal surface, but rather a random surface that exhibits fractal behavior.

> Many natural phenomena exhibit some form of statistical self-similarity that can be modeled by fractal surfaces. Moreover, variations in surface texture provide important

visual cues to the orientation and slopes of surfaces, and the use of almost self-similar fractal patterns can help create natural looking visual effects. The modeling of the Earth's rough surfaces via fractional Brownian motion was first proposed by Benoit Mandelbrot.

7.4   Fractals in Art

Fractals are used directly in many works of art. Even going back before the concept of fractal was popularized, the painter Jackson Pollock created paintings that display fractal characteristics, see the Wikipedia article on Jackson Pollack [98]. Today, many works of fractal-based art can be found on the Internet. For example, a search on "fractal art", "fractal art geometric" or "fractal art 3d" will return many fascinating works of art (many of which are animated).

Fractals are also used in architecture. Fractal architecture, given its use of patterns from nature, comes under the category of biophilic architecture, a type of architectural movement that seeks to connect people more closely to nature. The article entitled "The Aesthetic Appeal of Fractal Architecture" [99] provides an overview of the use of fractals in architecture and also provides some examples. Examples of fractal architecture include Hindu temples such as Kandariya Mahadev (Figure 134), Notre Dame Cathedral in Paris, City Hall in Bruges and Frank Lloyd Wright's ground plan for the Palmer House.

Credits for Figure 134 go to Paul Mannix, see https://commons.wikimedia.org/wiki/File:Khajuraho_-_Kandariya_Mahadeo_Temple.jpg. The original photo has been converted to grayscale.

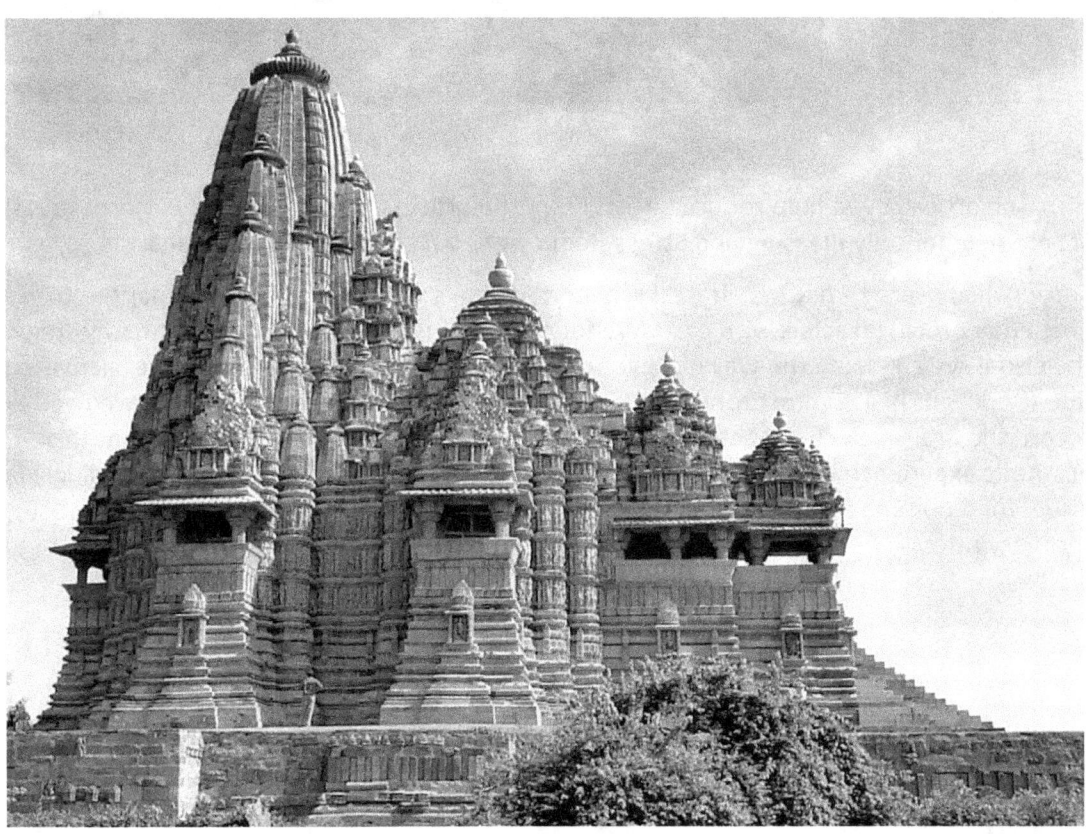

Figure 134. Kandariya Mahadeva Temple

Fractals can be used to create amazingly realistic landscapes. The first use of a fractal-generated landscape in a film was in 1982 for the movie "Star Trek II: The Wrath of Khan" to create an alien landscape. The Wikipedia article entitled "Fractal landscape" [100] provides further details on the topic. Figure 135 is a fractal landscape generated by Grome (an environmental modeling package developed by Quad Software).

Figure credits to Licu, see https://commons.wikimedia.org/wiki/File:Grome_canyon.jpg. The original image has been converted to grayscale.

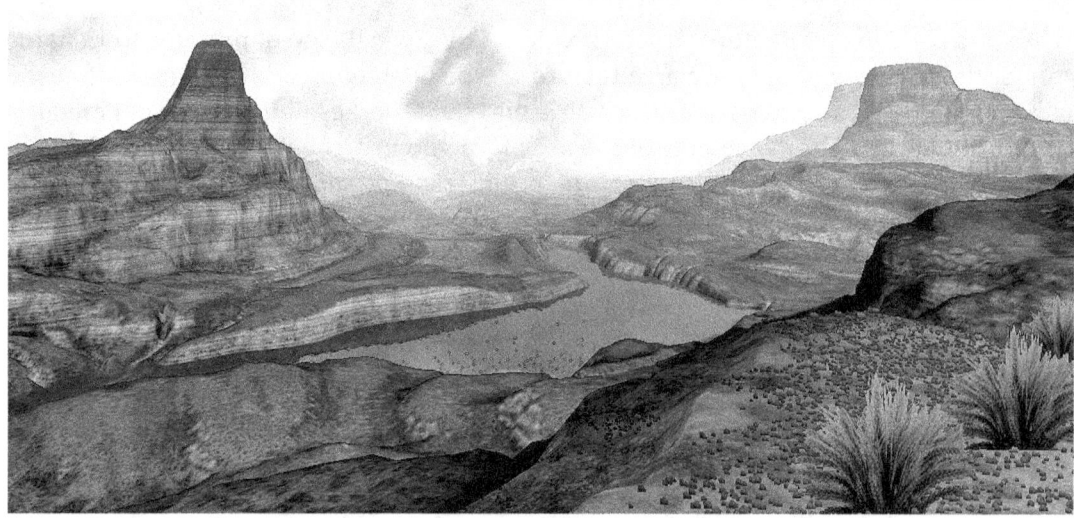

Figure 135. Fractal landscape

Fractal-based art can even help reduce stress. From the article entitled "Fractal Patterns in Nature and Art are Aesthetically Pleasing and Stress-Reducing" [101] in Smithsonian Magazine:

> Through exposure to nature's fractal scenery, people's visual systems have adapted to efficiently process fractals with ease. We found that this adaptation occurs at many stages of the visual system, from the way our eyes move to which regions of the brain get activated. This fluency puts us in a comfort zone and so we enjoy looking at fractals. Crucially, we used EEG to record the brain's electrical activity and skin conductance techniques to show that this aesthetic experience is accompanied by a stress reduction of 60 percent – a surprisingly large effect for a non-medicinal treatment. This physiological change even accelerates post-surgical recovery rates.

8   Proofs without Words

8.1   Overview

"Proof without Word" (sometimes referred to more accurately as "visual proofs") are proofs of mathematical theorems that are primarily based on a diagram (or several diagrams). Usually, some explanation is needed (so the "without words" part is not always true).

[**Author's Remark**: Some may question whether the diagrams in this section are to be considered art. I admit that one may need to have a mathematical background to appreciate some of the diagrams. Let the reader be the judge.]

[**Author's Remark**: While not related to mathematics, there is also something known as a wordless novel (basically a novel with only pictures). This reminds me of proof without words since in both cases a story is being told visually.]

8.2   Geometry

8.2.1   Pythagorean Theorem – Ancient Proof

The **Pythagorean theorem** states that the square of the hypotenuse of a right triangle equals the sum of the squares of the lengths of the other two sides of the triangle. There are many visual proofs of this theorem.

Figure 136 depicts a visual proof of the Pythagorean theorem. On the left, we see that the area of the large square is $(a+b)^2$ minus the area of the 4 identical triangles (each with area $\frac{1}{2}ab$) equals the sum of the 2 smaller triangles, i.e., $a^2 + b^2$. On the right, the larger square also has area $(a+b)^2$. Contained within the large square are the 4 triangles from the left figure. So, we have the area of the large square minus the areas of the 4 triangles must be equal to c^2. Comparing the two equations (written below each diagram in the figure), we see that $a^2 + b^2 = c^2$ which was to be proved.

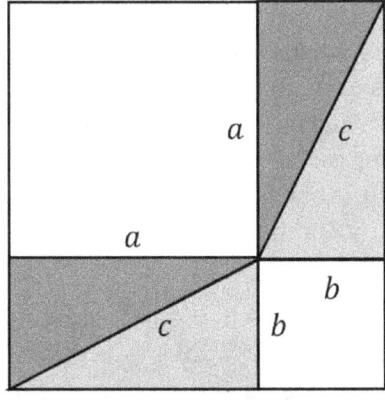

$$a^2 + b^2 = (a+b)^2 - 4\left(\frac{ab}{2}\right)$$

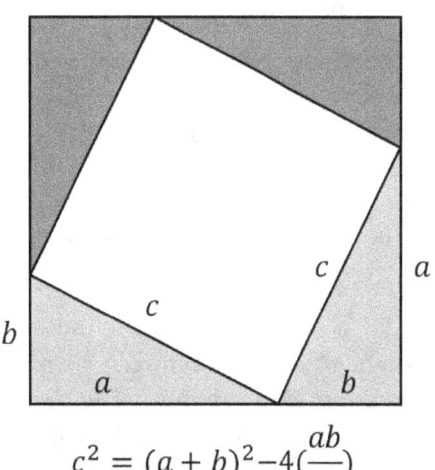

$$c^2 = (a+b)^2 - 4\left(\frac{ab}{2}\right)$$

Figure 136. Visual proof of Pythagorean theorem

The above proof is adapted from Chou Pei Suan Ching (aka Zhoubi Suanjing, a mathematical text dating from circa 200 B.C.

8.2.2   Pythagorean Theorem – President Garfield's Proof

James A. Garfield, the 20th president of the United States, provided a visual proof of the Pythagorean theorem while a member of the United States congress in 1876. His proof (with some explanation) is shown in Figure 137.

Garfield graduated from Williams College in 1856. He taught Greek, Latin, mathematics, history, philosophy, and rhetoric at Western Reserve Eclectic Institute, now Hiram College. Garfield also practiced law and was a brigadier general in the Civil War.

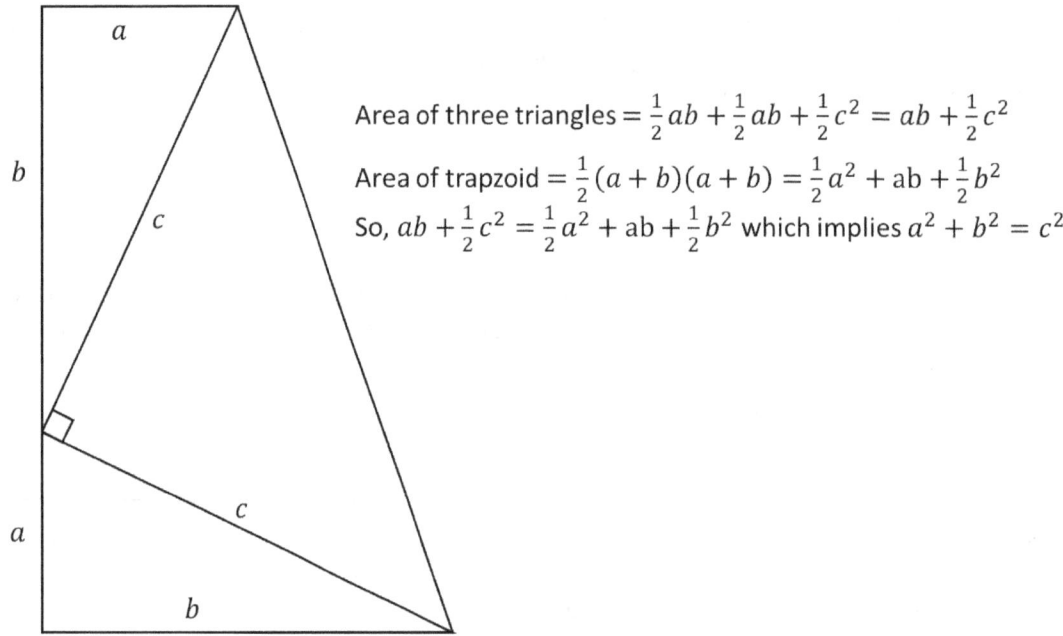

Area of three triangles $= \frac{1}{2}ab + \frac{1}{2}ab + \frac{1}{2}c^2 = ab + \frac{1}{2}c^2$

Area of trapezoid $= \frac{1}{2}(a+b)(a+b) = \frac{1}{2}a^2 + ab + \frac{1}{2}b^2$

So, $ab + \frac{1}{2}c^2 = \frac{1}{2}a^2 + ab + \frac{1}{2}b^2$ which implies $a^2 + b^2 = c^2$

Figure 137. United States President Garfield's proof of the Pythagorean theorem

8.2.3   Squaring the Circle

Squaring the Circle [102] (i.e., constructing a square whose area equals that of a given circle in a finite number of steps with only a compass and straightedge) is one of the three famous construction problems of antiquity. While many attempts were made, the problem remained open until 1882, when a solution to the problem was proved to be impossible by Ferdinand von Lindemann. However, the construction is possible with methods other than using only a compass and straightedge. The construction that follows was published by Thomas Elsner in Mathematics Magazine [103].

In Figure 138, a circle of radius one unit length is rolled one-half turn (180 degrees). This covers a distance equal to ½ the circumference of the circle, i.e., π. Below the horizontal line, a semicircle and square are drawn as shown. The claim is that the square and circle have the same area, i.e., 2π. [**Author's Remark**: Obvious? Well, it wasn't to me, but I was able to complete the thought with an additional diagram and some equations.]

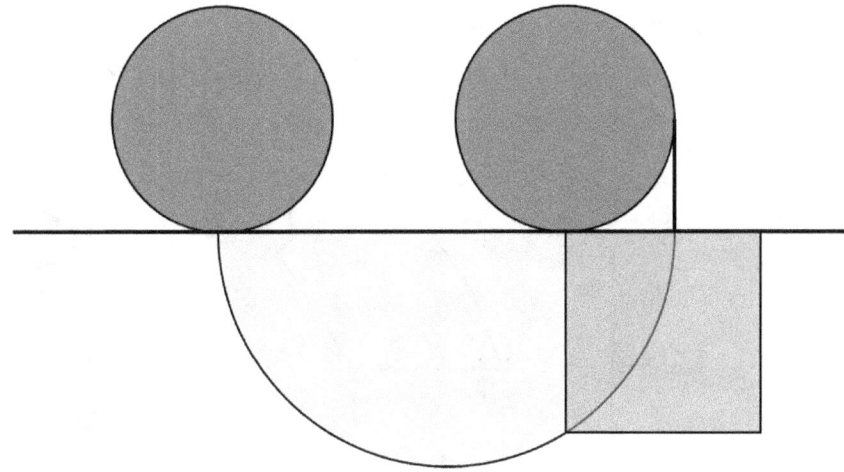

Figure 138. Construction of squaring the circle

Figure 139 adds a bit more detail. The key is the triangle shown in the semicircle. The diameter of the semicircle is $\pi + 1$ and so the radius of the semicircle as well as the hypotenuse of the said triangle is $\dfrac{(\pi + 1)}{2}$. The rest of the solution is explained in the figure.

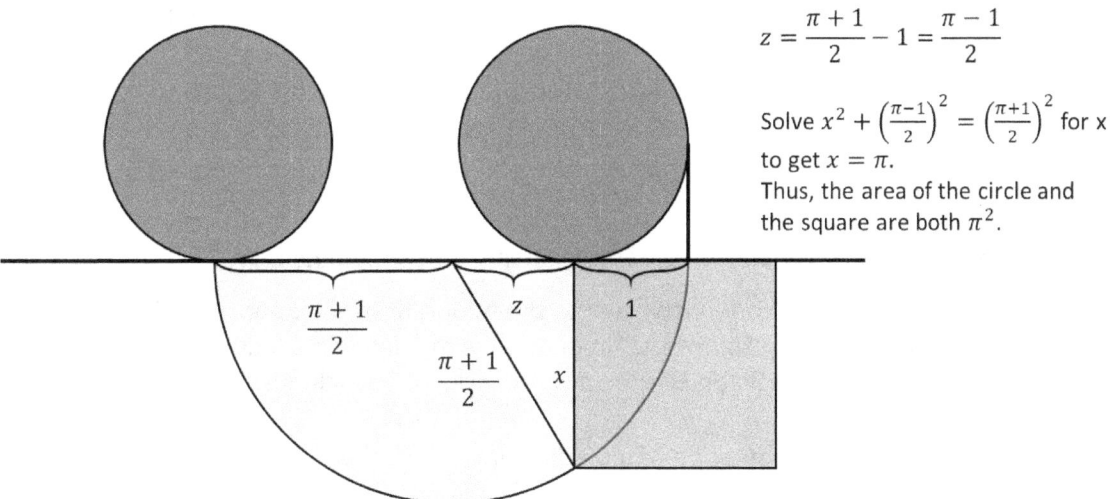

$$z = \frac{\pi + 1}{2} - 1 = \frac{\pi - 1}{2}$$

Solve $x^2 + \left(\frac{\pi-1}{2}\right)^2 = \left(\frac{\pi+1}{2}\right)^2$ for x to get $x = \pi$.
Thus, the area of the circle and the square are both π^2.

Figure 139. Construction of squaring the circle with further details

8.2.4 Arrangement of Triangles with Equal Area

The construction in Figure 140 comes from the book "Proofs without Words II" [104] (see the article entitled "Four Triangles with Equal Area" within this book). The proof is attributed to Steven L. Snover. The construction goes as follows:

- Start with the triangle at the upper left of the figure.

- Add squares off of each side of the triangle.

- At the upper left, triangles are added between the squats as shown.

- Remove the squares (bottom left).

- Rotate the outer triangles as shown.

The claim is that all four of the triangles in the final diagram (bottom right). Can you see why that is true?

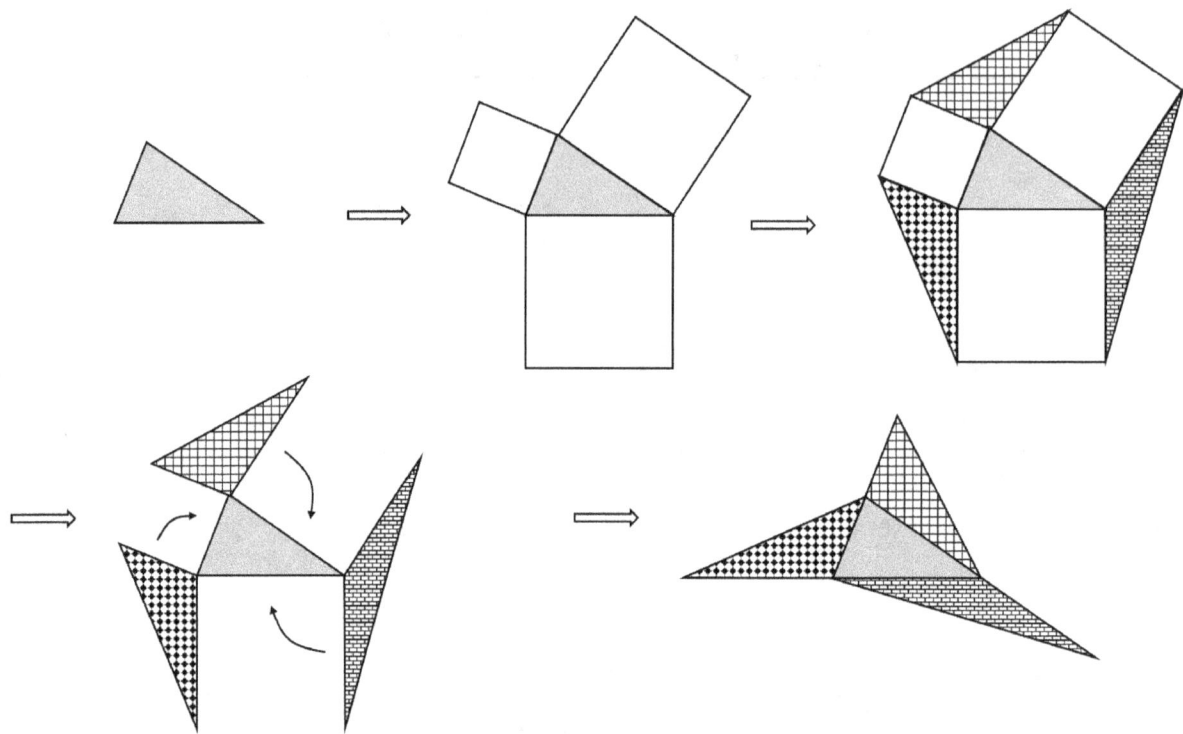

Figure 140. Configuration of triangles with equal area

[**Author's Remark**: It wasn't obvious to me. The following hint should help.]

A median line of a triangle goes from one vertex to the midpoint of the opposite side, e.g., DB is a median line of the triangle ADC in Figure 141. In general, a median line divides a triangle into two triangles of equal area. For example (in Figure 141), the area of triangle ABD and BCD are both of area $\frac{1}{2}h \cdot AB$ (noting that by the definition of a median line, $AB = BC$).

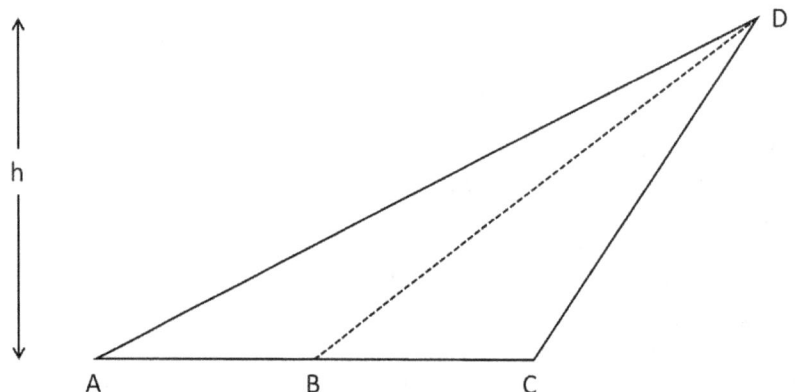

Figure 141. Median line divides triangle into triangles of equal area

8.2.5   Arithmetic Mean – Geometric Mean Inequality

The "inequality of arithmetic and geometric means" states that for non-negative real numbers a and b, the following holds true:

$$\frac{a+b}{2} \geq \sqrt{ab}$$

A proof of this theorem is shown in Figure 142. The proof comes from a note in Mathematics Magazine [105].

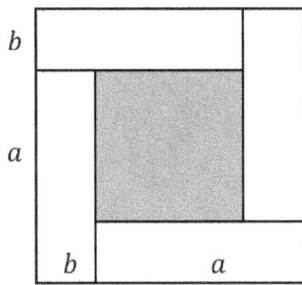

$$(a+b)^2 - (a-b)^2 = 4ab$$

$$\frac{a+b}{2} \geq \sqrt{ab}$$

Figure 142. Arithmetic Mean – Geometric Mean Inequality

8.3   Sums of Sequences

The following subsection involves various summation formulas for positive integers. According to the book "Proofs without Words" [106]:

- The visual proofs of the sum of positive integers (Section 8.3.1) and the sum of an ascending – descending integer sequence (Section 8.3.3) come from the ancient Greeks (original person unknown)

- The visual proof of the sum of positive odd numbers (Section 8.3.2) is attributed to Nicomachus of Gerasa (a Roman mathematician).

8.3.1 Sum of Positive Integers

Figure 143 gives a specific example of how to view the sum of integers. The integers from 1 to 6 are counted twice in the figure, and so the number of dots in the rectangle needs to be divided by 2 to get the correct answer. This leads to the more general formula:

$$1 + 2 + \ldots + n = \frac{1}{2}n(n + 1)$$

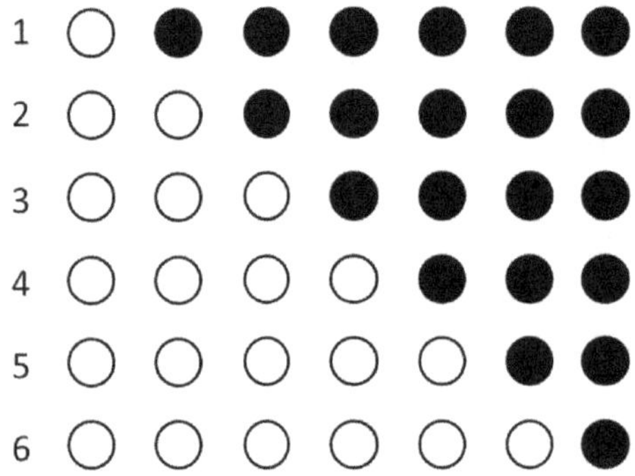

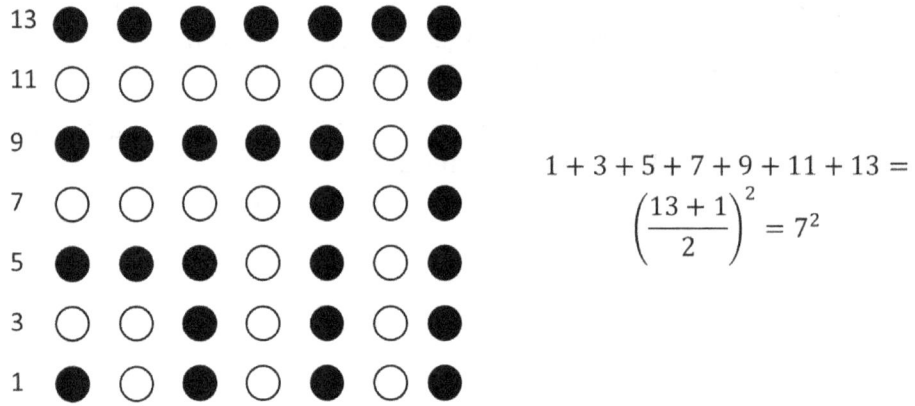

$$1 + 2 + 3 + 4 + 5 + 6$$
$$= \frac{1}{2}6(6 + 1)$$

Figure 143. Sum of positive integers

8.3.2 Sum of Positive Odd Integers

The sum of positive odd integers from 1 to 13 is shown in Figure 144.

$$1 + 3 + 5 + 7 + 9 + 11 + 13 =$$
$$\left(\frac{13 + 1}{2}\right)^2 = 7^2$$

Figure 144. Sum of positive odd integers

The general formula for the sum of positive odd integers is as follows:

$$1 + 3 + 5 + \ldots + (2n - 1) = n^2$$

8.3.3 Sum of Ascending – Descending Integer Sequence

The ascending and then descending sum of consecutive integers is equal to the square of the middle number in the sequence, noting that the middle number is not repeated in the summation. Several examples and a visual proof are depicted in Figure 145. The general formula is as follows:

$$1 + 2 + ... + (n-1) + n + (n-1) + ... + 2 + 1 = n^2$$

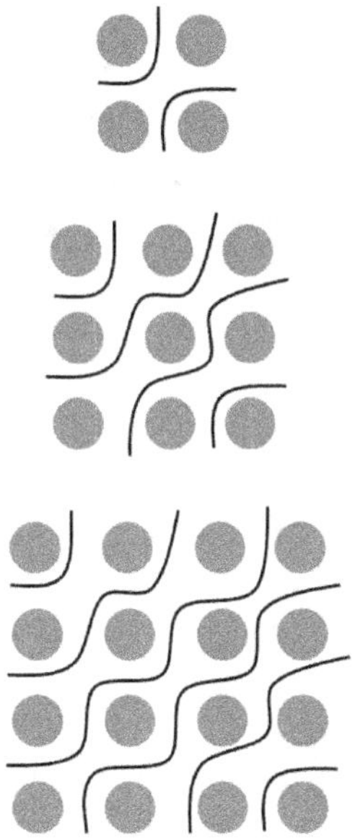

$$1 + 2 + 1 = 2^2$$

$$1 + 2 + 3 + 2 + 1 = 3^2$$

$$1 + 2 + 3 + 4 + 3 + 2 + 1 = 4^2$$

Figure 145. Sum of Ascending – Descending Integer Sequence

8.3.4 Sum of the Powers of Three

In order to visualize the sum of the powers of three, create each successive step by making three copies of the previous step and arranging the dots as shown in Figure 146. The source of proof is Page 108 "Proofs with Words II" [104], with attribution to David B. Sher.

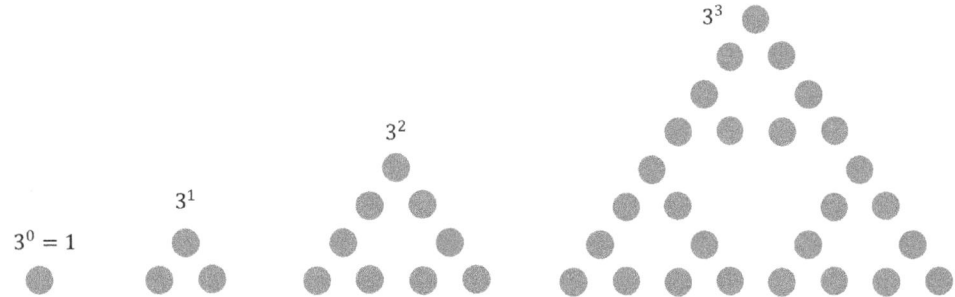

Figure 146. Sum of the powers of three - Part 1

Figure 147 shows two more steps in the process. The pattern is emphasized for the case of 3^5, i.e., if one removes the top dot, then 3^5 can be seen as two copies of all the previous powers of three. In general, the formal for the sum powers of 3 is

$$3^n = 2(3^0 + 3^1 + \dots + 3^{n-1}) - 1$$

Also, notice the resemblance to the Sierpinski triangle.

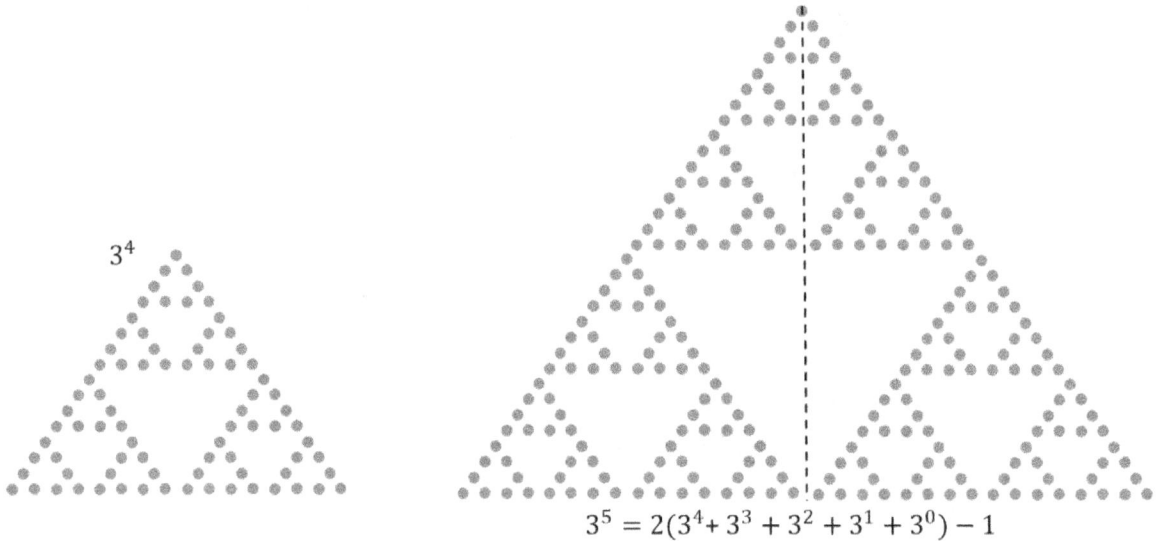

$$3^5 = 2(3^4 + 3^3 + 3^2 + 3^1 + 3^0) - 1$$

Figure 147. Sum of the powers of three – Part 2

Acronyms and Symbols

2D – Two dimensions (or dimensional)

3D – Three dimensions (or dimensional)

EEG – ElectroEncephaloGram

IFS – Iterated Function Systems

IH – IsoHedral

NASA – National Aeronautics and Space Administration

π – the symbol for the circumference of a circle divided by its diameter

References

[1]   Von Petzinger, G., *The First Signs: Unlocking the Mysteries of the World's Oldest Symbols*, Atria Books, 2017.

[2]   *Paleoanthropologist discovers set of geometric signs used around the world 40,000 years ago*, Ancient Code (online site), https://www.ancient-code.com/paleoanthropologist-discovers-set-of-geometric-signs-used-around-the-world-40000-years-ago, accessed on 12 December 2020.

[3]   Pickover, C., *The Math Book*, Sterling Publishing Co., Inc., 2009. '

[4]   Pollock, J., Number 1 (Lavender Mist), WikiArt, https://www.wikiart.org/en/jackson-pollock/number-1-lavender-mist-1950-1, accessed on 1 January 2021.

[5]   Mondrian, P., Composition No. 10, WikiArt, https://www.wikiart.org/en/piet-mondrian/composition-no-10-1942, accessed on 1 January 2021.

[6]   *Mathematics and art*, Wikipedia, en.wikipedia.org/wiki/Mathematics_and_art, accessed 11 December 2020.

[7]   *Tessellation*, Wikipedia, en.wikipedia.org/wiki/Tessellation, accessed on 13 December 2020.

[8]   *Regular Tessellations*, Wolfram MathWorld, https://mathworld.wolfram.com/RegularTessellation.html, accessed 13 March 2021.

[9]   *List of tessellations*, Wikipedia, en.wikipedia.org/wiki/List_of_tessellations, accessed 13 December 2020.

[10] Grunbaum, B., Shephard, G.C., *Tilings by Regular Polygons*, Mathematics Magazine, Vol. 50, No. 5, Page 227-247, November 1977.

[11] *Euclidean tilings by convex regular polygons*, Wikipedia, en.wikipedia.org/wiki/Euclidean_tilings_by_convex_regular_polygons, accessed on 4 September 2020.

[12] Swanson, I., *Quilting semi-regular tessellations*, available at http://people.reed.edu/~iswanson/semireg.pdf. In addition, this paper is the first three chapters of the book "Crafting by Concepts", edited by Sarah-Marie Belcastro and Carolyn Yackel, published by A K Peters.

[13] Fischer, M., *Tiling the plane with equilateral convex pentagons*, Parabola, Volume 52, Issue 3, 2016.

[14] Grunbaum, B., Shephard, G.C., *Tilings and Patterns*, W.H. Freeman and Company, 1987.

[15] *Hexagonal tiling*, Wikipedia, en.wikipedia.org/wiki/Hexagonal_tiling, accessed on 7 September 2020.

[16] *Marjorie Rice*, Wikipedia, en.wikipedia.org/wiki/Marjorie_Rice, accessed on 7 September 2020.

[17] Wolchover, N., *Pentagon Tiling Proof Solves Century-Old Math Problem*, Quanta Magazine, https://www.quantamagazine.org/pentagon-tiling-proof-solves-century-old-math-problem-20170711/, 11 July 2017.

[18] *Pentagonal tiling*, Wikipedia, en.wikipedia.org/wiki/Pentagonal_tiling, accessed 7 September 2020.

[19] *Math and the Art of M. C. Escher*, online wiki book with multiple editors, https://mathstat.slu.edu/escher/index.php/Math_and_the_Art_of_M._C._Escher, accessed on 7 September 2020.

[20] Hibma, T., *Aperiodic Rhomb Tiling*, https://www.aperiodictiling.org/wpaperiodictiling/index.php/fractional-rhomb-tilings/quarter-rhombs/, accessed on 14 December 2020.

[21] Penrose, R., *The role of aesthetics in pure and applied mathematical research*, Bulletin of the Institute of Mathematics and Its Applications, 10: 266ff, 1974.

[22] *Crystallographic restriction theorem*, Wikipedia, en.wikipedia.org/wiki/Crystallographic_restriction_theorem, accessed 10 September 2020.

[23] *Wallpaper group*, Wikipedia, en.wikipedia.org/wiki/Wallpaper_group, accessed 24 March 2021.

[24] Tile Decoration Alhambra Palace Spain Stock Photos, https://www.dreamstime.com/photos-images/tile-decoration-alhambra-palace-spain.html, accessed on 8 March 2021.

[25] Grünbaum, B., *What symmetry groups are present in the Alhambra?*, Notices of the American Mathematical Society (AMS) 53(6), http://www.ams.org/notices/200606/comm-grunbaum.pdf, 2006.

[26] Horne, C.E., *Geometric symmetry in patterns and tilings*, Published in North and South America by CRC Press LLC, 2000.

[27] Lenart M, *Construction problems as tiling puzzles*, *Design Studies*, 1989 10(1) 40–52.

[28] McLean, T.P., *Isohedral Tiling*, https://www.jaapsch.net/tilings/mclean/index.html, accessed on 16 September 2020. This article appears to only be available on the Internet and at that, it only survives at a mirror to the original site.

[29] *Perspective (graphical)*, Wikipedia, en.wikipedia.org/wiki/Perspective_(graphical), accessed on 20 October 2020.

[30] D'Amelio, J., Hohauser, S., *Perspective Drawing Handbook*, Dover Publications, Inc., 2004.

[31] *The History of Perspective*, article on the website "Essential Vermeer 3.0", http://www.essentialvermeer.com/technique/perspective/history.html, accessed 21 October 2020.

[32] *How to Draw a Building in 2-Point Perspective: Step by Steps*, YouTube video from Circle Line Art School, https://youtu.be/w_LbQviO1K4, accessed on 24 October 2020.

[33] *How to Draw using 3-Point Perspective: Simple Buildings*, YouTube video from Circle Line Art School, https://youtu.be/T4NBHkWe82k, accessed on 24 October 2020.

[34] *Projective geometry*, Encyclopedia Britannica, https://www.britannica.com/science/projective-geometry, accessed 25 October 2020.

[35] *Projective geometry*, Wikipedia, https://en.wikipedia.org/wiki/Projective_geometry, accessed 25 October 2020.

[36] Coxeter, H.S.M., *Projective Geometry (second edition)*, Springer-Verlag, 1987.

[37] Ayers, F., Schaum's Outlines: *Projective Geometry*, Schaum Publishing Company, 1967.

[38] Dhakal, B., *Desargues' Triangle Theorem*, YouTube video, https://youtu.be/2Z_zJaesLlw, accessed on 1 November 2020.

[39] *Pappus's Hexagon Theorem*, YouTube video from InfoSlide, https://youtu.be/vvwJHSvS_Ow, accessed on 1 November 2020.

[40] Adelson, E.H., *Lightness Perception and Lightness Illusions in The New Cognitive Neurosciences*, 2nd ed., M. Gazzaniga, ed. Cambridge, MA: MIT Press, pp. 339-351, (2000).

[41] *Trompe l'oeil*, Wikipedia, en.wikipedia.org/wiki/Trompe-l'œil, accessed on 1 January 2021.

[42] Seckel, A., *The Art of Optical Illusions*, Carlton Books Limited, 2000.

[43] *Impossible trident*, Wikipedia, en.wikipedia.org/wiki/Impossible_trident, accessed on 8 November 2020.

[44] *Penrose triangle*, Wikipedia, en.wikipedia.org/wiki/Penrose_triangle, accessed on 8 November 2020.

[45] *Waterfall (M. C. Escher)*, Wikipedia, en.wikipedia.org/wiki/Waterfall_(M._C._Escher), accessed on 8 November 2020.

[46] *White's illusion*, Wikipedia, en.wikipedia.org/wiki/White's_illusion, accessed on 8 November 2020.

[47] *Ebbinghaus illusion*, Wikipedia, en.wikipedia.org/wiki/Ebbinghaus_illusion, accessed on 8 November 2020.

[48] *Ponzo illusion*, Wikipedia, en.wikipedia.org/wiki/Ponzo_illusion, accessed on 9 November 2020.

[49] *Shepard tables*, Wikipedia, en.wikipedia.org/wiki/Shepard_tables, accessed on 9 November 2020.

[50] *Poggendorff illusion*, Wikipedia, en.wikipedia.org/wiki/Poggendorff_illusion, accessed on 1 January 2021.

[51] *Café wall illusion*, Wikipedia, en.wikipedia.org/wiki/Café_wall_illusion, accessed on 10 November 2020.

[52] *Hering illusion*, Wikipedia, en.wikipedia.org/wiki/Hering_illusion, accessed on 10 November 2020.

[53] *Kanizsa triangle*, New World Encyclopedia, https://www.newworldencyclopedia.org/entry/Kanizsa_triangle, accessed on 10 November 2020.

[54] *Fraser spiral illusion*, Wikipedia, en.wikipedia.org/wiki/Fraser_spiral_illusion, accessed on 11 November 2020.

[55] David, *Pinna's Intertwining Illusion*, https://www.opticalillusion.net/optical-illusions/pinnas-intertwining-illusion/, accessed on 11 November 2020.

[56] *Grid illusion*, Wikipedia, en.wikipedia.org/wiki/Grid_illusion#cite_note-Baumgartner-5, accessed on 11 November 2020.

[57] *Pinna illusion*, Scholarpedia, http://www.scholarpedia.org/article/Pinna_illusion, accessed on 11 November 2020.

[58] *Peripheral drift illusion*, Wikipedia, en.wikipedia.org/wiki/Peripheral_drift_illusion, accessed on 16 December 2020.

[59] Grovier, K., *Victor Vasarely: The art that tricks the eyes*, https://www.bbc.com/culture/article/20190305-victor-vasarely-the-art-that-tricks-the-eyes, accessed on 1 January 2021.

[60] Vasarely, V., *Zebra (1937)*, WikiArt: Visual Art Encyclopedia, https://www.wikiart.org/en/victor-vasarely/zebra-1937, accessed on 1 January 2021.

[61] *Boat (drawing)*, Wikipedia, en.wikipedia.org/wiki/Boat_(drawing), accessed 1 January 2021.

[62] Young, L.J., *Math Is Beautiful*, article from Science Friday, http://www.sciencefriday.com/articles/math-is-beautiful/, accessed on 2 January 2021.

[63] *Mathematical Concepts Illustrated by Hamid Naderi Yeganeh*, article from the American Mathematical Society (AMS), http://www.ams.org/publicoutreach/math-imagery/yeganeh, accessed on 2 January 2021.

[64] *The Illusion Only Some Can See*, YouTube video from Veritasium, https://youtu.be/dBap_Lp-0oc, accessed on 4 January 2021.

[65] *Ames trapezoid*, Wikipedia, en.wikipedia.org/wiki/Ames_trapezoid, accessed on 4 January 2021.

[66] *Amazing Animated Optical Illusions! #7*, YouTube video, https://youtu.be/UW5bcsax78I, accessed on 4 January 2021.

[67] *Anamorphosis*, Wikipedia, en.wikipedia.org/wiki/Anamorphosis, accessed on 5 January 2021.

[68] *Amazing Anamorphic Illusions!*, YouTube video from brusspup, https://youtu.be/tBNHPk-Lnkk, accessed on 5 January 2021.

[69] *23 Amazing Anamorphic Artworks That Need A Mirror Cylinder To Reveal Their Beauty*, online article from deMilked, https://www.demilked.com/anamorphosis-anamorphic-cylinder-art/, 5 January 2021.

[70] *Animation basics: The optical illusion of motion*, TED-ed talk, https://youtu.be/V8A4qudmsX0, 5 January 2021.

[71] *Coordinate system*, Wikipedia, en.wikipedia.org/wiki/Coordinate_system, accessed on 20 November 2020.

[72] *Cardioid*, Wikipedia, en.wikipedia.org/wiki/Cardioid, accessed on 20 November 2020.

[73] *Geodesic polyhedron*, Wikipedia, en.wikipedia.org/wiki/Geodesic_polyhedron, accessed on 21 November 2020.

[74] *Polygonal number*, Wikipedia, en.wikipedia.org/wiki/Polygonal_number, accessed on 23 November 2020.

[75] *Pascal's triangle*, Wikipedia, en.wikipedia.org/wiki/Pascal's_triangle, accessed on 24 November 2020.

[76] *Patterns in Pascal's Triangle*, article in *Cut the Knot*, http://www.cut-the-knot.org/arithmetic/combinatorics/PascalTriangleProperties.shtml, accessed on 24 November 2020.

[77] *Voronoi diagram*, Wikipedia, en.wikipedia.org/wiki/Voronoi_diagram, accessed on 25 November 2020.

[78] Mansurov, N., *What is Moiré and How it Can Ruin Your Photos*, article in Photography Life, https://photographylife.com/what-is-moire, accessed on 25 November 2020.

[79] Rule of thirds, Wikipedia, en.wikipedia.org/wiki/Rule_of_thirds, accessed on 4 January 2021.

[80] Stewart, J., *Images Reveal How Perfectly Ansel Adams' Photos Align With the Golden Ratio*, online article from My Modern Met, https://mymodernmet.com/ansel-adams-golden-ratio/, accessed on 4 January 2021.

[81] *List of works designed with the golden ratio*, Wikipedia, en.wikipedia.org/wiki/List_of_works_designed_with_the_golden_ratio, accessed on 4 January 2021.

[82] *Importance of Golden Ratio in Architecture*, online article from The Arch Insider, https://thearchinsider.com/importance-of-golden-ratio-in-architecture/, accessed on 4 January 2021.

[83] Hibma, T., *Koch Tiles*, https://www.aperiodictiling.org/wpaperiodictiling/index.php/2x2-supertiles/koch-tiles/, accessed on 1 December 2020.

[84] Sol, J., *The Mandelbrot Set: How it Works, and Why it's Amazing!*, YouTube video, https://youtu.be/2JUAojvFpCo, accessed on 1 December 2020.

[85] *List of fractals by Hausdorff dimension*, Wikipedia, en.wikipedia.org/wiki/List_of_fractals_by_Hausdorff_dimension, accessed on 2 December 2020.

[86] *Weierstrass function*, Wikipedia, en.wikipedia.org/wiki/Weierstrass_function, accessed on 3 December 2020.

[87] *Almost everywhere*, Wikipedia, en.wikipedia.org/wiki/Almost_everywhere, accessed on 3 December 2020.

[88] *Cantor function*, Wikipedia, en.wikipedia.org/wiki/Cantor_function, accessed on 3 December 2020.

[89] *Do all fractals have this property?*, discussion thread on StackExchange – Mathematics, https://math.stackexchange.com/questions/2675954/do-all-fractals-have-this-property, accessed on 3 December 2020.

[90] *Minkowski's question-mark function*, Wikipedia, en.wikipedia.org/wiki/Minkowski%27s_question-mark_function, accessed on 3 December 2020.

[91]   Krieger, H., *The Mandelbrot Set – Numberphile*, YouTube video, https://youtu.be/NGMRB4O922I, accessed on 4 December 2020.

[92]   *Introduction to Complex Numbers*, Khan Academy, YouTube video, https://youtu.be/SP-YJe7Vldo, accessed on 4 December 2020.

[93]   *Logistic map*, Wikipedia, en.wikipedia.org/wiki/Logistic_map, accessed on 5 December 2020.

[94]   *This equation will change how you see the world (the logistic map)*, YouTube video from Veritasium, https://youtu.be/ovJcsL7vyrk, accessed on 5 December 2020.

[95]   Prusinkiewicz, P., Lindenmayer, A., *The Algorithmic Beauty of Plants*, http://algorithmicbotany.org/papers/#abop, accessed on 5 December 2020.

[96]   *L-system*, Wikipedia, en.wikipedia.org/wiki/L-system, accessed on 5 December 2020.

[97]   *L-Systems - The Nature of Code*, YouTube video from The Learning Train, https://youtu.be/f6ra024-ASY, accessed on 5 December 2020.

[98]   *Jackson Pollock: Fractal computer analysis*, Wikipedia, https://en.wikipedia.org/wiki/Jackson_Pollock#Fractal_computer_analysis, accessed on 6 December 2020.

[99]   Woolfe, S., *The Aesthetic Appeal of Fractal Architecture*, https://www.samwoolfe.com/2020/04/the-aesthetic-appeal-of-fractal-architecture.html, accessed on 7 December 2020.

[100] *Fractal landscape*, Wikipedia, en.wikipedia.org/wiki/Fractal_landscape, accessed on 7 December 2020.

[101] Taylor, R., *Fractal Patterns in Nature and Art Are Aesthetically Pleasing and Stress-Reducing*, Smithsonian Magazine, https://www.smithsonianmag.com/innovation/fractal-patterns-nature-and-art-are-aesthetically-pleasing-and-stress-reducing-180962738/, accessed on 6 December 2020.

[102] *Squaring the circle*, Wikipedia, en.wikipedia.org/wiki/Squaring_the_circle, accessed on 8 December 2020.

[103] Elsner T. (1977). *The Rolling Circle Squares Itself*, Mathematics Magazine, 50 (3) 162. DOI: 10.2307/2689507.

[104] Nelsen, R.B., *Proofs without Words II*, The Mathematical Association of America, 2000.

[105] Schattschneider, D., *Proof without words: The arithmetic mean – geometric mean inequality*, Mathematics Magazine, Vol. 59, No. 1, Page 11, February 1986.

[106] Nelsen, R.B., Proofs without Words, The Mathematical Association of America, 1993.

Index of Terms

www.ingramcontent.com/pod-product-compliance
Lightning Source LLC
Chambersburg PA
CBHW081514220526
45467CB00010B/2914